ISAAC ASIMOV
Writer of the Future

World Writers

ISAAC ASIMOV
Writer of the Future

William J. Boerst

MORGAN
REYNOLDS
Incorporated

Greensboro

ISAAC ASIMOV *Writer of the Future*

Copyright © 1999 by William J. Boerst

Photo credits: p. 53 From *Pebble In The Sky* (Jacket Cover) by Isaac Asimov. Used by permission of Doubleday, a division of Bantam Doubleday Dell Publishing Group Inc. p. 89 Copyright©1977 by Davis Publications, Inc., reprinted by permission of Dell Magazines, a division of Crosstown Publications.

Library of Congress Cataloging-in-Publication Data
Boerst, William J.
  Isaac Asimov : writer of the future / William J. Boerst. —
    p. cm. — (World writers)
  Includes bibliographical references and index.
  Summary: Describes the life and career of the prolific writer who is known for writing nearly 500 books of both science fiction and non-fiction.
  ISBN 1-883846-32-3
    1. Asimov, Isaac, 1920 -   —Juvenile literature. 2. Authors, American—20th century—Biography—Juvenile literature. 3. Scientists—United States—Biography—Juvenile literature. [1. Asimov, Isaac, 1920 -   . 2. Authors, Americans.]
    I. Title II. Series.
PS3551. S5Z575 1998
813' .54—dc21
[b]

                                                              98-29407
                                                                   CIP
                                                                    AC

Printed in the United States of America
First Edition

CONTENTS

Chapter One

Growing Up Different

The tall, thin high-school freshman raised his hand. Isaac Asimov was eager to read his essay aloud in front of the class, and was pleased when his teacher selected him to read. But, after only two paragraphs, the teacher interrupted the reading and sent Isaac back to his seat.

Isaac had eagerly signed up for the course in writing. He had been writing on his own for years, and thought he already knew his craft. The essay he had been so proud of described a country scene filled with the scent of flowers, something that as a resident of New York City he knew little about. Later, Isaac realized that he should have written about what he knew: rugs being shaken out of open windows in Brooklyn; the laughter of children as they played punchball in neighborhood streets. His mistake had been in choosing a high-sounding topic and language that had little to do with his own experiences.

The facts of Isaac's early life experiences were certainly interesting enough to make a lively essay. He was born in Petrovichi (pronounced Pe-TROO-vi-chi), Russia, in January 1920. In search of a better life, the family of four—three-year-old Isaac, his parents, and his young sister

Marcia—moved to the United States. A small boat took them from Russia to Liverpool, England, where they boarded the ocean liner *Baltic* for their trip to the U.S.

Isaac remembered that on the ship a sheet was placed against a wall and a movie shown on it. That was the first movie he had ever seen.

On February 3, 1923, the *Baltic* arrived in New York. Ellis Island was their first stop. This was where all immigrants to New York City had to enter the United States. The Asimov family waited in a very large room full of talking and yelling people. Most spoke languages other than English. Isaac and his father got separated from his mother and Marcia, and his father panicked. Rushing around trying to find the missing two, he discovered that new arrivals were routinely separated according to sex. At Ellis Island, Isaac developed a fever and a cough. By the time he felt bumps inside his mouth and his parents noticed a skin rash, it became clear that Isaac had the measles. This meant that the family would have to remain on Ellis Island a few days. February 7, the family got back together again, along with their sponsor, Uncle Joe Berman of Brooklyn.

The immigrants had to learn new customs. In Petrovichi, there had been no indoor plumbing. It was common practice to urinate into street gutters. One time Isaac stood on the curb of a Brooklyn street and did the same. A woman sitting on a folding chair nearby moved away, muttering. His parents had not instructed young Isaac about the change.

The young boy learned English by asking older boys what signs said and how alphabet letters were sounded. By age five he had taught himself to read.

Once, trying to impress Uncle Joe, Isaac's father said,

"Isaac can find any word in the dictionary."

Joe uttered, "Impossible!"

Five year old Isaac thought that was the word he was to look up, so he found it in the dictionary.

Isaac's father never raised a hand to strike his children, but Isaac's mother did. She had a fiery temper and struck the children quite often. She also struck out verbally, using very colorful language. One time, Isaac repeated some of the phrases in front of his father, who asked, shocked, "Isaac, where did you hear such terrible words?"

Isaac answered, "Mamma says it all the time."

Isaac and his younger sister Marcia did not get along. Arguments became shouting matches. The busy parents had little time to help settle differences. His mother ran up the stairs, shouting, "Stop fighting!" Then she lectured them on how they were the worst behaved children in the neighborhood.

After his fifth birthday, Isaac went to kindergarten. He and a neighbor girl walked off for their first day with handkerchiefs pinned to their shirts so that they wouldn't wipe their noses on their sleeves. His mother thought that a full year of kindergarten would be a waste of Isaac's time. She convinced the school authorities Isaac had been born September 7, 1919, instead of January 2, 1920. (The parents really didn't know his exact date of birth.) Isaac advanced to first grade half way through his kindergarten year. After about a month in the first half of first grade, Isaac was moved to the second half. He really didn't want to move ahead because he liked his teacher. He cried, but the teacher patted .his hand and said he had to go. The next day, when he tried to go back to her, she took his hand and led him out.

Isaac's neighborhood was a busy place. In the morning, pushcart owners lined up to peddle their fish or vegetables or needles and thread. The iceman was a regular visitor to households. He chopped large blocks into cubic feet with his pick, then lugged the sixty pounds up stairs to fill iceboxes. Children's outdoor games varied with the time of year. At one point everyone played with marbles, at another tops or checkers. Girls played jacks, a game in which they bounced a ball and picked up metal objects called jacks. Boys used checkers to play skelly. At each corner of the sidewalk squares, they chalked off smaller numbered squares of varying sizes. The center part was called the skelly (possibly short for skeleton). The object was to flick your checker into the one square, then the two, and so on. The shooter earned a second shot if he landed in the right square or hit an opponent's checker. If he landed between a large square and a small square without touching a line, he went back to square one. Isaac played this game for hours at a time.

The boys also played punchball, a variation on baseball. Whenever Isaac went out to play this, his father would say, "Are you going out to play with those bums again?" He believed that if Isaac played in the streets, he would end up no good. He wanted Isaac to study or read or think noble thoughts.

Because he didn't get to play punchball very often, Isaac did not develop as a player and was not in demand for the boys' teams. He worked out his own ball games to play by himself. In one, he would throw a ball against a wall or stair flight. One bounce back meant zero points. A missed ball ended the game. A return without a bounce earned one point.

The goal was to get as many points as possible before a game ended.

Isaac's father had worked as a knitter in a sweater factory, manning one of the machines. He had also done door-to-door sales. He was not good at that because he tended to argue his own strong opinions. Then, in 1926, when Isaac was in the second grade, he invested his savings into a Brooklyn candy store. In addition to candy, the store stocked such items as sodas, newspapers, and cigarettes. This was a move up. Isaac's father was his own boss. But it meant long hours—6:00 a.m. until 1:00 a.m. He could not do this himself. It was a family business. His wife worked the earlier shift, going to bed early at night to be ready for the next morning. Mr. Asimov always took a nap from 2:00 to 4:00 P.M. so that he could stay open until closing.

Because the candy store required long hours, Isaac ate most meals alone. Here is where he picked up the habit of reading at meals. Family members were almost never together except in the store. Isaac always knew where his parents were, though. His mother tended to be over-protective. If Isaac were late getting home, she imagined the worst possible trouble.

Family life was centered around the store. There was little social time. Isaac did not do without one piece of it, however—the movies. Every Saturday afternoon his mother gave him a dime and sent him across the street to the theater for three hours. Because it was a children's matinee, the place was filled with the noise of yelling and laughing children. The serials of fantastic adventures with many fight scenes, masked villains, and cliffhanger endings were the favorites. All movies were silent at this time. Isaac loved the excitement and confusion of those Saturday afternoons.

Beginning in second grade, he developed the habit of rapidly reading all his textbooks in the first few days of school. That way, he didn't have to study during the rest of the school year. He did homework as fast as he could soon after he returned home each day. Usually his grades were good. No matter what grades he got, though, his father thought he should improve.

Grades were rarely a problem; behavior almost always was. A fast learner, Isaac always had time to talk with students in neighboring desks. This got him into trouble with teachers. One time Isaac brought home a report card with A in academics but a B+ in "deportment." Since his mother didn't know what the word deportment meant, she visited the school to talk with Isaac's teacher, who explained that Isaac "talked a little bit too much." His mother marched him home and spanked him, but that didn't help him reform.

Some teachers supported Isaac despite his behavior. His fifth-grade teacher was nice to him. Even though his sixth-grade teacher had a reputation for meanness, she took a special liking to Isaac. That may have been because he was bright or because he showed no fear of her.

Isaac began to notice that he was different from other pupils. He learned everything the first time through. Most other students needed constant repetition. He also had a retentive memory. As soon as he was exposed to something new, it stayed with him. Once he knew he was unusual, he did not hesitate to remind others of this fact. At first the older, bigger, slower boys beat him because he showed off. Then Isaac singled out the biggest one and did his homework for him. This bought him safety.

Jules Verne was one of the early science fiction writers.

July 25, 1929, when he was nine years old, his mother gave birth to another boy. Isaac had the chance to help name his baby brother. He chose the name *Solomon*. His mother may have wanted to avoid the stigma of a Jewish name. She chose Stanley, later shortened to Stan.

Around this time, Isaac discovered the science-fiction pulp magazines sold in his father's store. His father would not let Isaac read the cheap pulp magazines with titles like *Thrilling Detective* and *Weird Tales*; he thought they were trash not worthy of his smart son. But Isaac discovered that a new science-fiction magazine had the word *science* in its title—*Science Wonder Stories*. His father agreed to let Isaac read a magazine with the word science in the title. Soon Isaac was reading the other science-fiction magazines.

Issac soon discovered that *Astounding Science Fiction* was his favorite science-fiction magazine. The stories in *Astounding* were wildly imaginative, using ideas adapted from the new discoveries in science, especially physics, to create action-filled stories of travel through and beyond our solar system. In a hugely popular novel called *The Skylark of Space* by E.E. Smith, serialized in *Astounding* at the time Isaac began reading the magazine, young scientists discover a new energy source that allows them to explore thousands of light years beyond our solar system. Other stories drew on the new physics of Einstein and others to extrapolate not only the possibility of time travel, but to also suggest that it was possible to go back and interfere with the space-time continuum. In another serialization in *Astounding*, *The Legion of Time* by Jack Williamson (who later became a friend of Issac's), the premise is that the future of the human race depends on whether a twelve-year-old boy picks up a rusty magnet from the dirt. In these stories no event or idea is too tiny or too large. The only limitations were the imaginations of the reader and the writer.

Isaac soon wanted to begin telling stories of his own. At first, to entertain his friends, he retold tales he had read in science-fiction magazines. It was during these storytelling sessions that Isaac discovered he enjoyed performing. Then he began writing stories. Feeling that he lacked the scientific background, he didn't dare attempt science-fiction. Instead, he wrote a series book that he called *The Greenville Chums at College*. In one evening he wrote two chapters. The next day he told the story to his friends. Not knowing he was the author, they asked to read the book when he was finished reading it. He began to take himself more seriously as a writer.

The candy store left little time for play. His slight build meant that in any rough games Isaac got the worst of it, making him dislike violent sports. He made books his escape. He could read a few paragraphs during slow times at the store. In later years, he insisted that his becoming a bookworm was a conscious choice with no bitterness attached: he enjoyed his books and would have found a mere social life unpleasant.

Chapter Two

Apart From Others

In 1932, Isaac graduated to senior high school. His father wanted him to become a medical doctor. Attending ordinary public high school made it difficult for a Jewish boy to be accepted into a college or university pre-med course. Boys High School of Brooklyn carried more prestige than the neighborhood high school. Isaac applied there and was accepted. He attended classes in a building called Waverly Annex. When the school newspaper editor asked for a reporter from the Annex, Isaac volunteered.

Later, Asimov realized why that freshman writing course had been so much trouble. He was spending all his out-of-school time working in his father's candy store, so he did not have experiences to draw on that other fourteen-year-olds might. Also, he did not understand contemporary literature of the 1930s because his leisure-time reading, except for science-fiction, had been in nineteenth-century works.

The main assignments of the course were submitted to the school's literary magazine. Most students wrote pieces that contained sadness and realism. Determined to be different, Isaac chose a humorous essay, which he entitled

"Little Brothers." He tried to pattern the piece after a famous essayist he admired named Robert Benchley.

To Isaac's delight, his composition was accepted for publication in the literary magazine. The teacher sneered as he announced to the class, "It was the only thing anyone submitted that was supposed to be funny, and I had to have something funny." But that did not discourage Isaac. For him, the course immediately turned from a failure into a worthwhile venture.

Isaac was becoming aware of all the ways he was different from his schoolmates. For example, he preferred enclosed places. Windowless display rooms in department stores appealed to him, as did newsstands in subway stations. He pictured a subterranean newsstand boarded over with a light and cot inside so that he could lie there and read to his heart's content. The back room of his father's store, a curtain drawn across the opening, gave Isaac a feeling of safety. He developed other fears—the fear of being late, of getting lost.

When Isaac began reading newspapers, he discovered the world of baseball statistics. He loved anything with the flavor of New York, and here were two teams representing his city—the Giants and the Yankees. He spent hours listening to the radio. He set up charts for both major leagues, working out all the percentages and standings even though they would be in the newspaper the following day. Most of the store customers were Brooklyn Dodger fans and he enjoyed debating with them. Isaac's father did not like this bantering; he was afraid it would drive away business.

Summer evenings were perfect times to get acquainted with girls. One girl called Mazie lived across the street. She was a year older than Isaac. He thought she was beautiful. He hung around her stoop and sometimes went to the movies with her.

As he walked from place to place, Isaac was often lost in thought. He didn't notice people, even if they were relatives or family friends. Sometimes customers felt snubbed and told Isaac's parents. They lectured him about proper manners.

Walking home from the library was especially hazardous. He could check out three books at a time. People would often see him with a book under each arm, reading the third as he walked along sidewalks and crossed streets. One time, walking home in a snowstorm, he became so engrossed in the falling-snow patterns that he kept staring up. When he got home, his mother was furious because a customer had reported to her. He had seen Isaac walking with his head up toward the sky and his mouth open.

Isaac loved cemeteries. Not far from his apartment house were three. He liked the peace and quiet. Cemeteries were like parks minus the people. They were like those enclosed rooms that he cherished. He felt lighthearted walking through them. Once when he was walking through a cemetery, the caretaker asked him not to whistle because mourners got upset.

Isaac didn't just whistle in cemeteries. He whistled wherever he went. This too was reported to his mother. She scolded him. He just went right on being himself with no intention of changing his eccentric habits.

Since Isaac was in an accelerated program, he became a high-school senior when he was fifteen. Looking ahead toward college, his father bought him a used typewriter.

Mazie from across the street, an accomplished typist, introduced Isaac to the basics of typewriting. At first he single-spaced on both sides of the paper using no margins; eventually he learned to double-space on only one side of a sheet, but he never did master margins.

His first fiction on the typewriter was a fantasy—forty pages,on both sides, single-spaced, with no margins and, finally, no ending. This cured him of writing fantasy for some time. The next short story, possibly written in 1936, was his first attempt at science-fiction. Like the fantasy, it got bogged down after considerable length and died. Despite these setbacks, Isaac loved writing. It was unpredictable. He made up his stories as he wrote, rarely planning ahead. He only planned the central problem and a possible solution to it. This was a method he continued to use as he grew older. When he began this story writing, he was thinking of publishing as a distant dream.

When it came time to go to college, Isaac applied to Columbia College, an ivy league school in New York. He was granted an interview. It did not go well. Nervousness caused him to be overly talkative, which made him seem immature. The interviewer did not grant admission to Columbia College, but he did suggest Seth Low Junior College, part of the large Columbia system. There Isaac could improve his chances for admission to Columbia College when he became a junior. Isaac knew he could not afford Seth Low and therefore would have to attend City College.

In the fall of 1935, Isaac began at City College. Three days into the semester, he received a letter from Seth Low asking why he had not registered. His father called the registrar's office and explained that they could not afford the tuition. The person at the other end offered a one-hundred-dollar scholarship and a job earning fifteen dollars a month. Isaac immediately switched schools.

Isaac wanted to make a better impression in college than he had in high school. He was determined to leave behind his disciplinary problems. He had trouble with his hair, however. One time the director of the college called Isaac into his office, took out a comb, and combed Isaac's hair. Apparently Isaac hadn't been combing his hair often enough during the day to appear neat.

Zoology became Isaac's major. In his first course, he had to dissect worms, frogs, and fish. At one point, each student was to find a homeless alley cat, take him to the lab, chloroform him, and dissect him. The Asimov family had always liked cats. They were in the habit of adopting strays. Isaac hated what he had to do, but he did it.

Another incident in the course helped sour Isaac on zoology. The teacher lectured in a room with a tile floor. During one lecture, Isaac took out a handkerchief to blow his nose. A glass marble rolled out of his pocket onto the floor making an obvious noise as it bounced and rolled down the aisle. The professor waited until the marble had stopped, then said, "Well, this is a *junior* college." Everyone laughed.

Isaac took his first chemistry course and loved it. The teacher was intriguing, and the lab work and demonstrations were challenging. Isaac found the work easy. Perhaps he had gotten a head start. During a high-school chemistry course, he had read chemistry texts from the public library.

Embryology, another zoology course, did not go well. Isaac looked through his microscope at chicks in various stages of development. He rarely saw what he was supposed to see. Even if he could see it, he had trouble drawing it. During a class the professor announced that everyone was passing "except one."

Isaac asked nervously, "Who's the one?"

The professor kindly replied, "Strange you should ask that," and got laughter from the class.

Isaac was able to squeak by with a final embryology grade of C-. But the combination of incidents—the cat, the marble, and the lab failure—prompted his decision to change majors. He began to wonder whether he should pursue the medical career his father had always wanted for him.

As a college sophomore, Isaac held a part-time job assisting in the psychology department. The professor was attempting to create a chart that would be helpful in statistical research. Others involved in the project complained that Isaac was too bossy. The professor told Isaac to stop trying to take over the project. Embarrassed, Isaac asked for a transfer to another project. He knew his ability to get along with others was limited. He found it difficult to take orders; but he loved to give them, having others follow his commands.

The chart later disappeared and the project had to be abandoned. Isaac reflected that if he had remained in charge, the project would have been completed. He often grinned with self-satisfaction and thought to himself, "Serve you right!"

A graduate student asked Isaac for help developing a maze to be used to test students. A board was wired with nail-heads. If you touched any of the nails with the stylus, either a red or a green light would flash on. The object was to complete the maze lighting only the green lights. When Isaac learned the path rapidly, the student assumed that he had created too easy a maze. After making some changes, he returned to Isaac for another test run. This time Isaac had more difficulty reaching the end of the maze. The graduate student assumed that now the puzzle was all right for average students.

At the presentation of his project the psychology professor asked the graduate student, "Why is it so complicated?"

"It has to be, or it's solved too easily," the graduate student explained.

"Did you check it on someone?"

"Certainly."

"On whom?"

Pointing to Isaac, the student answered, "On him."

The professor had the graduate student redo the project, testing it on others so that it would come out somewhat simpler.

After the graduate student had left, Isaac apologized to the professor, saying, "If I had known he was looking for an average student, I'd have *told* him I was above average."

"It's all right," said the professor. "You're below average in plenty of ways." Isaac was discovering that intelligence could be a curse as well as a blessing.

Chapter Three

The World of Science Fiction

If Isaac had doubts about a medical career, he had none about science-fiction. He collected stacks of science-fiction magazines. On May 29, 1937 he started to work on his first short story, "Cosmic Corkscrew." He hoped to get it published. The next year Isaac began keeping a diary.

Isaac wrote letters to the magazine *Astounding Science Fiction*. To his surprise, the editors printed them. On the day *Astounding* was supposed to arrive at the store, Isaac would wait impatiently. Then, one day no copies arrived. He panicked. Had the magazine gone out of business? Isaac called the publishers to make sure the magazine was still alive and was assured that it was. The next week, still no *Astounding*. When he visited the Manhattan offices to ask what was wrong, an employee explained that the publication date had been changed and the store would get its bundle the next week. Sure enough, the following week *Astounding* arrived. Instead of studying for final exams, Isaac pored through back issues.

He realized that he was hooked on reading science-fiction. He also wanted to write it. Actually, as he recalled years later, his goal was becoming much more specific:

"What I wanted was to write a *science-fiction* story and to have it appear in a *science-fiction* magazine." He wanted to see his name alongside the other authors he had read so avidly. He was determined to be published. Visiting the offices of the publisher made the magazine seem more within reach.

After a year sitting idle, his short story "Cosmic Corkscrew" went back into the typewriter. Once he finished it, he had no idea how to proceed. His father suggested that Isaac deliver the manuscript to *Astounding* in person.

In June 1938 Isaac walked into the offices of *Astounding* and asked to see the editor. After a brief phone conversation, the secretary said, "Mr. Campbell will see you." Isaac could not believe her words. He had expected to be thrown out of the building. She led him through a room filled with paper rolls and magazine piles to another smaller room. There sat the editor, John W. Campbell.

John Campbell had started out in science-fiction as a writer, publishing stories under his own name and under the pseudonym Don A. Stuart. (One of his stories, "Who Goes There?," was the basis for the classic horror movie *The Thing.*) After assuming editorship of *Astounding* in 1937, he stopped writing his own stories and concentrated on editing. Campbell's particular gift was to extract the most interesting ideas or themes from the stories that writers submitted to him and to encourage them to rewrite with these new ingredients as the center. Writers who were willing to follow his suggestions often went on to have great success writing science-fiction. In addition to Isaac, other writers whose careers Campbell helped to launch were Lester del Rey, Robert Heinlein, and L. Ron Hubbard.

Isaac always credited John Campbell with being a major influence on his writing career. (Photo by Jay Kay Klein)

In Campbell's office that day the young, loud aspiring writer and the most important editor in science-fiction talked for over an hour. Campbell shared future issues of the magazine with Isaac, assuring him that it was not dying. He recalled that when he was seventeen, his own father had sent one of his manuscripts to *Amazing Stories*. It would have been published except for two accidents: the company lost the original, and Campbell had no carbon copy to send. He thanked Issac for bringing his story by and promised to read it quickly and to respond in writing.

Two days later Isaac received his first rejection letter. He wrote in his diary, "At 9:30 I received back 'Cosmic Corkscrew' with a polite letter of rejection." Far from being sad, Isaac pushed ahead, determined to meet with Campbell again. His second attempt at a short story was not accepted either. But that did not discourage him. In his diary he wrote: "... it was the nicest possible rejection you could imagine. Indeed, the next best thing to an acceptance. He told me the idea was good and the plot passable. The dialog and handling, he continued, were neither stiff or wooden...and ...there was no one particular fault but merely a general air of amateurishness, constraint, forcing. The story did not go smoothly. This, he said, I would grow out of as soon as I had sufficient experience. He assured me that I would probably be able to sell my stories but it meant perhaps a year's work and a dozen stories before I could click...."

As a writer, Isaac wanted to get published. His diary entries became shorter and less detailed so that he could spend more time on short-story writing. From that first conversation with Campbell, Isaac concentrated on writing for publication.

The 1930s were the great era of pulp-fiction magazines. Before television, people would often spend leisure time reading fast-paced stories in magazines with titles like *Thrilling Detective*, *Weird Tales*, and Isaac's favorite, *Astounding Science Fiction*. Magazine fiction writers were paid by the word, so it didn't make sense to spend a lot of time on one story. Isaac established a rapid, professional routine that he used throughout his career. Each piece went through two stages—first draft, then final copy. After two typings, if the piece was not good enough, Isaac concluded that it was not worth redoing.

He got other rejections and had every reason to be discouraged, but his monthly visits with Campbell kept his spirits up.

Isaac wrote one magazine, asking what had happened to his submission. An editor wrote back that the magazine was accepting it. This was October 1938. By January 1939 he had written ten stories. Nine he had submitted to Campbell of *Astounding*. Eight of those nine had been rejected; one sale was pending. He had also submitted seven to other magazines. Ten stories written, submitted sixteen times, resulting in one sale that netted sixty-four dollars.

Campbell made a suggestion that startled and encouraged Isaac—rework a story to make a minor idea the main focus. Isaac had never before rewritten for an editor, only to please himself. In three weeks he had the rewrite completed. The project gave him satisfaction. He felt he now had the story half-accepted. Then copies of the magazine containing his first published short story arrived.

At Campbell's suggestion, Isaac worked through three revisions of another story. After waiting two weeks and hearing nothing, he visited the *Astounding* offices. Campbell said, "Oh, yes, your story? You haven't got it yet?" Isaac thought he meant that the manuscript was being returned. Then Campbell added, "It's up in the accounting room now," meaning the check. This was Isaac's second sale to Campbell in almost two years.

Meanwhile, Isaac's father still wanted him to become a doctor. As a college senior, Isaac applied to five New York City area medical schools. All five rejected him. Becoming a doctor seemed doubtful. Isaac was not sad. He decided he would apply to graduate school in the field of chemistry.

In September 1939, Isaac enrolled as a graduate student in the chemistry department at Columbia. His high ability as measured by tests did not match up with his average performance in the classroom. In fact, his academic performance had gone from outstanding in public school, to somewhat brilliant in undergraduate school, to average in graduate school. He figured that his outspoken behavior got in the way of class work. He was especially awkward in the lab part of science courses, unable to find the things under the microscope that he was supposed to observe.

Isaac didn't let this declining performance discourage him. Academic achievement was simply one measuring stick. He knew he was gathering a broad base of knowledge through his work in school and library.

In class Isaac sat next to an attractive twenty-one-year-old blond woman named Irene. He liked her immediately. She was brighter in science than he was. Isaac decided he was in love. He waited for her at the university library. He followed her when he had a good enough excuse. During Christmas break, he arranged to meet her in Manhattan for a date. He gave her candy. They ate in a cafeteria and saw *The Hunchback of Notre Dame* at Radio City Music Hall. This first date took place on his twentieth birthday.

Once at lunch Irene called him the "cleverest" fellow she knew. They walked home with their arms linked. He felt as if he were in heaven. Another time, when they went to a movie and then a planetarium, they held hands. Standing next to the chemistry building on campus, Isaac asked her to hold his books so he could tie his shoelace. Instead, he quickly kissed her on the corner of her lips. As she handed back his books, she said, "That was mean," but did not seem upset.

After she earned her master's degree, she accepted a job in Wilmington, Delaware. On their last date before she moved away, visiting the World's Fair, Isaac suggested a roller-coaster ride. He had a secret motive. If Irene became scared, she would hang on tight to him and he could steal a kiss. Isaac realized too late that he himself was afraid of heights. He clung to her until the terror was over. She had no problem with either the ride or Isaac's panic.

Once Irene had moved to Delaware, Isaac felt desperate. He recalled the experience in his autobiography: "Heartbreak, as I judge from my limited experience, is the pain one feels at the loss of a love object, in the case where the love object, not returning the love, breaks off (whether kindly or cruelly) and disappears. The person you love is gone, but still exists, and is simply not available....For a long time, I wandered about unsmiling and unhappy. For me, the clouds hovered close and sunshine was meaningless. I somehow couldn't think of anything but the young woman, and when I did think of her there was a constriction of the chest and I found it difficult to breathe. I decided there was no meaning to life and I was quite, quite, *quite* certain that I would never get over it. In fact, I wasn't sure it might not be a good thing to simply lie down and die of heartbreak. The odd thing is that I did get over it and I don't remember exactly how."

John Campbell had made changes in one of Isaac's stories before publishing it. At Campbell's suggestion, Isaac had distinguished between Africans/Asians and Americans/ Europeans. In the published version of the story, Campbell had added several of his own paragraphs showing Earthlings' superior ability to make war. Isaac did not like the type of changes that Campbell had made. Campbell's insistence on the superiority of humans to every other potential alien race reminded him of the recent Nazi takeovers in Europe. Although he admired Campbell as an editor, Isaac did not accept the elder man's more conservative political beliefs. Although he wasn't religious, Isaac was Jewish, and his family had immigrated to the United States. Campbell's view of native-born Americans as always superior to other nationalities, was simply not acceptable to Issac.

As he developed into a writer, Isaac tried not to be as controlled by Campbell's ideas as he had been in the beginning of their relationship. He sometimes agreed to Campbell's suggestions, but then tried to ignore them or change them as he rewrote. One way he accomplished this was to leave aliens out of his plots so there couldn't be a contrast between aliens and humans. Another was to write about robots, since he had no trouble showing humans' superiority to robots.

Isaac had difficulty getting started with his first robot

story. After four false starts, he went to Campbell, admitting that he couldn't get going. Campbell advised, "Asimov, when you have trouble with the beginning of a story, that is because you are starting in the wrong place, and almost certainly too soon. Pick out a later point in the story and begin again." Isaac did what was suggested and it worked.

Isaac decided he needed a plan for his robot stories. In discussions, Isaac and Campbell developed a set of three laws to govern a robot's behaviors. Isaac reworded them slightly to read as follows:

1. A robot may not injure a human being or through inaction allow a human being to come to harm.
2. A robot must obey the orders given it by human beings except where such orders would conflict with the First Law.
3. A robot must protect its own existence as long as such protection does not conflict with the First or Second Laws.

In 1941, Isaac took qualifying exams to enter Columbia's Ph.D. program in chemistry. He did not qualify. While he did earn his master's degree, he could not yet be a candidate for the Ph.D. He could, however, continue to take courses and try again the next year. He wondered whether certain professors might have voted him down, figuring he was not Ph.D. material.

One day Asimov had to register for the military draft; the next day he registered for a summer course at Columbia University. Between listening to the radio for war news and attending classes six days a week, he did not have much time for his short-story writing. He was also dating girls. On one occasion he did not return home until five o'clock in the morning. His mother was shocked, but his father defended Isaac's late hours

Asimov was trying to think of a new story idea. Opening a book to any page, he did free association on the first words his eyes met. It was a play in which a Queen threw herself at the feet of guards. Thinking of guards, he then thought of the military, military campaigns, empires, and the Roman Empire.

An idea formed in Isaac's mind of a future history, told by someone looking back over the events of the story. At Campbell's office, he was excited with his new idea. Campbell wanted Asimov to think in grander terms—a series of longer stories portraying the fall of a First Galactic Empire, the dark time following it, and then rise of a Second Galactic Empire. He told Isaac to "go home and write the outline." Isaac tried the outline but couldn't create one. Finally, he began writing without it. He never was able to work from outlines, whether it was for fiction or nonfiction. This was the beginning of the Foundation stories.

Another story Isaac wrote was suggested to Campbell by a quotation from the American philosopher Ralph Waldo Emerson: "If the stars should appear one night in a thousand years, how would men believe and adore; and preserve for man generations the remembrance of the city of God . . ."

Campbell said he thought mankind would go mad if the stars only appeared once every thousand years. He encouraged Isaac to go home and write a story around this idea.

Isaac typed the quotation from Emerson at the top of a sheet of paper and began writing. Before he was finished he had a thirteen-thousand-word story entitled "Nightfall."

Nightfall

By Isaac Asimov

"If the stars should appear one night in a thousand years, how would men believe and adore, and preserve for many generations the remem-

The title page from the first publication of Isaac's groundbreaking story "Nightfall," in the September 1941 issue of *Astounding Science Fiction*.

When it was published in *Astounding,* it created a sensation and was quickly added to most people's list of favorites. Thirty years after its initial publication as a feature story, fans and critics voted "Nightfall" the best science-fiction story ever published. Only three years after first visiting Campbell's office, Isaac had grown into a highly accomplished science-fiction writer. He was only twenty-one.

Isaac was also slowly learning to get along with others. At one point, his graduate advisor warned him that his noisy singing during lab sessions was disturbing other students. They had complained to Professor Thomas. Isaac decided to visit Thomas for a chat. Accused of the singing, Asimov explained, "I'm not in chemistry to make a living, sir. It's not my bread-and-butter. I'm going to make money writing. I'm in chemistry because I love it. It's my cakes-and-ale, and I can't help singing when I'm working. I'll try to stop, sir, but it will be an effort. It's no effort not to sing for those who complain. I don't imagine they like their work." After that, the two were friends. Even so, he cut out the singing in the lab.

On Sunday, December 7, 1941, Isaac had just finished writing a story and was relaxing by listening to the radio. His father was in the next room napping. Suddenly there was a news bulletin: the Japanese had attacked Pearl Harbor. Running into his father's room, he shook him and yelled, "Pappa, Pappa!"

His father sat up and said, "What's the matter?"

Isaac said, ""We're at war. The Japanese have bombed us." Usually his father complained about being awakened, but not this time.

Assuming that he would not be accepted as a Ph.D.

candidate at Columbia, Isaac applied to and was accepted in New York University's graduate chemistry program. He would still prefer to go to Columbia, but he was convinced he would not be accepted. A friend bet Isaac a dollar, against Isaac shaving off a new mustache, that Isaac would make it into Columbia's Ph.D. program. On the day before acceptances were to be announced, Asimov hung around Columbia in the hope of sniffing out the results. Professor Thomas smiled and advised, "Go home and write a story. I can't tell you the results, but don't worry too much." Another professor said, "I can't tell you the results, but don't worry too much." Isaac kept questioning teachers until finally one said: "You passed." He could start Columbia in 1942, after he shaved off his mustache.

Chapter Four

Love and War

A friend arranged a double date. When Isaac saw his date, Gertrude Blugerman, he was impressed. He recalled in his autobiography that "she was five feet, two inches in height, a trifle on the plump side . . . with beautiful dark hair, and even more beautiful dark eyes, a generously proportioned figure—and most of all—was the very image of Olivia de Havilland, who, in my opinion, was the most beautiful actress in Hollywood." He asked her out several times after that.

As Isaac began his research for the Ph.D., war loomed ahead. Many graduate students were leaving the university and accepting positions as civilians working for the government. Asimov decided to do the same. He got hired at the Philadelphia Navy Yard at a salary of $2,600 a year, a good salary for the time. He did not want to leave his research, but there was a good chance that he would be drafted. Furthermore, he was becoming more serious about Gertrude. Regular pay would allow him to consider marriage.

Seven weeks after they met, Isaac approached Gertrude with the idea of marriage. She seemed willing. Nine days later, however, she told him she did not love him and would not see him again. Desperate, Asimov talked and talked until he got back into her favor. This time, he made his own rule not to mention marriage. Eventually she accepted the idea. They set the date for seven weeks after his new job began.

At Philadelphia Navy Yard, Isaac discovered that his fellow lab workers were concerned about being drafted. They were being reclassified every six months. It became a waiting game. But the work itself had variety. He tested products to be used on airplanes and made sure that such items as cleaners, soaps, and seam sealers met Navy specifications.

June 26, 1942, Isaac and Gertrude were married. Neither family was religious, so getting the services of a rabbi proved difficult. Only the immediate families attended, and the ceremony was held in the Blugerman living room. When the rabbi chanted Hebrew, Gertrude did her best not to laugh. As a requirement, he asked for a witness not of either family to come forward. There was none. Gertrude's father went into the apartment-building hall and grabbed someone passing through. Another requirement was that the witness be wearing a hat, which he was not doing at the time. The rabbi grabbed Isaac's father's hat and placed it on the confused witness's head. Toward the end of the ceremony, the rabbi was about to smash a glass under his heel. Mr. Blugerman snatched the glass from his hand to avoid a messy floor.

Gertrude changed Asimov's hygiene habits. He shaved every day instead of every other. He took showers each morning, not just when he felt like it. He used deodorant regularly. But she could not change his unruly hair. No matter how carefully he combed, by the end of the day it was a mess.

Isaac returned to writing in his spare time. He finished three stories and sent them off to Campbell. All three were accepted.

At work in the Navy Yard, he had to write reports on lab-test results. Each one was to be written in Navy style, a formal system in which every paragraph had to be numbered or lettered as in an outline. Under *I* or *II* Asimov had to write a subdivision using capital letters. Under *A* or *B* he had Arabic numerals. Under *1* or *2* he wrote small letters. Under *a* or *b* he put Arabic numerals in parentheses. And so on. In addition, every sentence had to be cross-referenced with other sentences that referred to it elsewhere. So at the end of a sentence he might have a reference that would read *II, C, 3, a, (1)*.

In creating one final report, he divided all the parts, some as far as *[(a)]*. He also cross-referenced nearly every sentence, making fun of Navy style. He considered the piece a nightmare to read and expected it to be returned for a rewrite. But the joke was on him. Superiors considered the writing an outstanding job and began using this report as a model for good Navy writing. Asimov grinned and shook his head in amazement.

The monotony of his job was alleviated somewhat because fellow science-fiction writers Robert Heinlein and Sprague de Camp, both John Campbell discoveries, also worked in the Navy Yard. The three men met often and talked over story ideas.

Isaac loved to develop routines in his life. On Saturday nights after supper, he bought the early editions of two Philadelphia Sunday papers. After he had showered, he made a large glass of hot chocolate and put out a half pound

(From left) Robert Heinlein, L. Sprague de Camp, and Isaac at the Philadelphia Navy Yard in 1944. (photo credit: U.S. Navy)

of cookies. Beginning with the comics, he read both papers at a leisurely pace, dipping the cookies in the hot chocolate. In later years, he often remembered those Saturday nights with fondness.

Another memorable routine occurred when Asimov and Gertrude visited their families in New York during the summer. The two of them would walk slowly up and down the boardwalk at Coney Island. They might buy souvenirs or play games or eat food. It was comfortable to walk a mile or two without fighting automobile traffic.

As his fourth Foundation story came out in the October 1944 issue of *Astounding*, Asimov was becoming tired of the series. He wanted a change. His next story, also part of the Foundation series, was based on his experiences in the Yard. It explored the red tape of bureaucratic life. Part of it contained letters written in Navy style.

The possibility of being drafted continued, although war was coming to an end. Asimov's classification of 2BL (limited by nearsightedness) was scheduled to end soon. April 15, 1945, three days after the death of President Franklin Roosevelt, he received a six-month extension of his draft deferment. May 8 was V-E (Victory in Europe) Day. If he could keep from being drafted until his twenty-sixth birthday (seven months), he would probably avoid the draft because males over twenty-six were considered too old. When Asimov had just five months to go till his twenty-sixth birthday, the Draft Board reclassified him to 1AB (the *B* for nearsightedness), making him eligible for the draft.

The afternoon of August 6, Asimov was reading a book while Gertrude ironed clothes. Suddenly a voice interrupted the regular radio broadcast to announce that the United

States had dropped an atomic bomb on Hiroshima. This ended World War II. Even so, Asimov received his draft notice September 7, 1945.

He traveled to Philadelphia for his induction. The first evening in the service, left alone with time on his hands, Asimov became almost unbearably homesick. Even though he did not normally attend Jewish Sabbath services, he sought out the chapel just to be with others and to keep busy. The service helped: when he returned to his bunk, he promptly fell asleep.

The next night Asimov got his first Army job—emptying ashtrays and trashcans and sweeping floors at the officers' club. He realized then that this really was the Army.

He went by train to Fort Meade, near Baltimore, Maryland, where he would undergo aptitude tests. Asimov realized that this was the first time he was traveling without family and against his will. As he watched telephone poles pass on the landscape outside, he kept saying to himself, "I can't change my mind. I can't get off the train. I can't go back home. I've got to go wherever I'm told. I have no say in the matter."

He spent part of his tour at Camp Lee, Virginia, the other part in Hawaii, where he got a temporary assignment as a clerk-typist. At some point during the stay in Hawaii, Asimov underwent a major personality change. Until now, he had showed off his superior intelligence. Some people were bothered by this trait, but he could not resist it. One day, some soldiers were talking about how an atomic bomb worked. They were getting it wrong, and Asimov prepared to set them straight. Suddenly, he thought, *Who appointed you their educator? Is it going to hurt them to be wrong about the atom bomb?* He returned to a book he was reading. He had tired of being disliked. As a rule, he tried to restrain himself from that time on.

After eight months, one-third of the usual two-year hitch, Isaac was discharged to continue his important Columbia University research on enzymes. He had left Columbia for the Navy Yard at age twenty-two; he was returning at age twenty-seven. The war had interrupted a university career, but the story writing and publishing had continued. He placed "Nightfall," in a short-story collection called *Adventure in Time and Space*. This was his second story to be put into an anthology. Anthologizing was a way for a story already published in pulp magazines to earn money again. It gave Asimov hope for a possible career in writing.

He may have learned to not antagonize people with his intelligence. But his tendency toward absent-mindedness could still be embarrassing. When the couple got a bill for twice what the other tenants were paying, he went directly to the gas-company office. Furious, he said, "See here, we have never used enough gas to bring us up to the minimum. We have no children. We both work. We cook perhaps four meals a week. How can we possibly get a bill for $6.50? I *demand* an explanation."

The clerk answered, "You really insist on an explanation?"

"Certainly," Asimov said "if you can think of one besides general incompetence."

"Fortunately," he said, "I can think of one. This is an electric bill."

Asimov had to present a seminar about his research. He was to explain what he was doing and why. Then he was to accept questions from the audience. The seminar would become a sharing session, supporting the idea that Columbia's chemistry department housed a community of learners. In reality, however, lecturers often talked over the heads of most listeners, boring them.

Isaac wanted his seminar to be interesting. He prepared carefully, placing formulas on the blackboard before anyone else arrived. He progressed steadily through his lecture, not having to interrupt the talk with notes because they were already on the board. The audience liked the presentation. His advisor thought it was the most understandable seminar he had ever attended.

He continued his research experiments. When he put the compound called catechol in touch with a water surface, it dissolved immediately—so fast, in fact, that Asimov didn't even see it touch the water before it disappeared. He wondered, *What if it dissolves just before it hits the water?* What an exciting idea for a science-fiction story! Then he would remember that soon he would have to write his dissertation in very formal, stilted language. It would be like writing the Navy Yard letters in outline form, or even worse than that. Why couldn't he write a mock dissertation about such a compound as a science-fiction story? He could have some fun writing in the dreaded academic style. Campbell encouraged him to go ahead.

Ironically, Asimov was having trouble adjusting to a nonfiction writing style for his dissertation. He liked to write rapidly. His advisor, Dr. Dawson, insisted on weighing each sentence and thinking how it could be restructured for greater clarity. For example, Asimov made frequent reference to a constant called M. Finally Dawson stopped during a reading and asked, "What is *M*?"

Asimov replied, "Why, you know what it is, Dr. Dawson. It's [the] mixing time."

"Why don't you say so?"

Defending himself, Asimov explained, "But Dr. Dawson, if I say so *now*, I kill the suspense."

"Isaac, Dawson said, "I hate to break the news to you, but you're not writing one of your science-fiction stories."

"You mean I have to define *M*?"

"The instant you first use it."

Much later, as his dissertation was being considered by a committee, one professor said with disapproval, "It reads like a mystery story."

Asimov had entered Columbia at age fifteen. Now, at twenty-eight, he was still there. But this was his last year in the doctoral program. He would have to make career plans. Job interviews were not plentiful, and they were leading nowhere. In addition, his fiction-writing progress had been slow. Eventually, landed a job for the next year. He would receive a salary of $4500 as a postdoctoral assistant to one of the professors, working on an improved medication for malaria.

As the time approached for the publication of his mock dissertation, "Endochronic Properties of Resublimated Thiotimoline," in *Astounding*, Asimov became nervous. He did not want this take-off on the serious work of chemists to anger his dissertation-committee professors. He asked Campbell to publish his story under a pseudonym. Campbell agreed, but forgot the agreement at time of publication. When the story was published, a friend in the lab said, "Hey, that was a funny satire on chemistry by you in the new

Astounding, Isaac."

Asimov asked, "What makes you think the article was by me?"

The labmate paused, then said, "Well, when I noticed your name on it, I thought, 'Gee, I'll bet he wrote it.'"

Another labmate said: "Don't tell me you put your own name on a satire of chemistry when your dissertation is coming up?"

In 1948, Asimov finished his dissertation. Seventy-four pages long, it was called "The Kinetics of the Reaction Inactivation of Tyrosinase During Its Catalysis of the Aerobic Oxidation of Catechol."

The doctoral candidate had to present an oral defense of his research. He knew that there are two inappropriate types of responses to the questions the professor's would ask him. One was to freeze and not answer the question. The other occurs when the student is able to do nothing but sit and laugh hysterically. Asimov was into the second mode. He entered the room giggling nervously.

One professor asked how Asimov knew that his enzyme came from the mushroom he claimed. Asimov said that the enzyme came from grocery-store mushrooms.

"So what?" the professor probed.

"So *Agaricus campestris* is the only species sold in the grocery store."

"How can you be sure of that?"

Thinking fast, Asimov said, "If I had had any doubts, sir, I would have referred to a text on mushrooms."

"Whose?"

"Yours." There was only one problem with this answer. The professor had never written any text on mushrooms.

After an hour and twenty minutes of questioning, one of the professors asked the final question: "What can you tell us, Mr. Asimov, about the thermodynamic properties of the compound known as thiotimoline?" Recognizing the allusion to his fictional dissertation published in *Astounding*, Asimov dissolved in laughter and had to be helped from the room. Five minutes later, the professors shook his hand and said, "Congratulations, Dr. Asimov." Isaac had finally earned his Ph.D. Now the question was, "What was he going to do with it?"

Chapter Five

Farewell Campbell, Hello Boston

Isaac spent his twenty-ninth birthday brooding that he would soon be thirty. He was also disheartened about both his careers. Even with his Ph.D. he did not have regular employment. His university assistantship could end at any time. He had always thought he possessed special talent to offer others. Now he felt like a failure. His writing was also going slowly. He did not enjoy the story he was working on, the last of his Foundation series. While a fourth story had been put into an anthology, no book-length manuscripts had found publishing outlets.

As the year wore on, however, both areas began to look brighter. Some employers were showing interest. Johns Hopkins University in Baltimore, Maryland wanted him to come for an interview. Boston University also asked to see him. Trying to be his agent, Asimov's friend Fred Pohl worked to interest the publishing company Doubleday in a book-length version of his story "Grow Old With Me." Isaac was doubtful, but Fred advised, "Who cares about *your* opinion? Let's see what Doubleday thinks." Asimov agreed.

While the Johns Hopkins job failed to materialize, Boston University Medical School offered an instructorship starting at $5000 a year, including a one-month vacation with pay. One of his jobs would be to teach freshman biochemistry. Asimov accepted the offer. Fred Pohl succeeded in getting an offer from Doubleday for "Grow Old with Me." The manuscript would have to be lengthened from 40,000 to 70,000 words. However, the company immediately gave an unconditional advance of $150. If they liked the revision, they would then pay $350 more, which Asimov could keep regardless of final acceptance or rejection.

Asimov began to feel that his relationship with John Campbell at *Astounding* was a mixed blessing. He had been working closely with the editor since 1938. In the eleven years, seven of them at the top of the science-fiction-writing pyramid, he had earned an average of $700 a year—not enough to live on. But his mentor had also channeled Asimov into a narrow terrain so that he had trouble expanding. Asimov seemed to be a one-editor writer. How much of this success was due to himself, how much to the editor? What if something happened to Campbell? What would happen to Asimov's market?

Isaac knew that writing was not the problem. He had worked hard to develop a concise and clear prose style that was perfect for telling the type of science-fiction he wrote. His problem was finding time to think up his stories. The thinking time was what couldn't be rushed. Most of a writer's time is spent thinking, not writing.

All these doubts were in Isaac's head when he attended a 1949 lecture given by the chemist Linus Pauling. It was a stunning speech on science, and it reminded the struggling author of a friend's earlier remark that Asimov himself was a good explainer. He also remembered the success he had delivering his lecture in graduate school. Maybe he could use this talent for explanation to further his writing career. He wrote an article, "Detective Story for Non-chemists," that dealt with how chemists work out formulas. Campbell rejected it for *Astounding,* although that magazine did sometimes publish nonfiction articles.

On May 29, 1949, the editor Walter Bradbury of Doubleday accepted the book manuscript for "Grow Old With Me." He requested that Asimov change the title to *Pebble in the Sky,* which sounded more like science-fiction.

Preparing for the move to Boston to take the teaching job, the Asimovs sublet a small apartment sight unseen. This was their seventh move since marriage. Once they saw the dingy apartment, they knew there would have to be an eighth move soon. The furniture was old and lifeless. The shower water was hot or cold, depending on how much the other tenants had used. A refrigerator was not furnished; they had to buy their own.

Isaac was working on a new novel entitled *The Stars, like Dust,* but it was not going well. Earlier, Walter Bradbury of Doubleday had encouraged him to create an outline and the first two chapters. Now Brad returned them to Asimov with no contract. He said that he would give an advance of $250 but wanted six or seven chapters before a contract could be offered. The six or seven chapters could not include the first two Asimov had done. They were not acceptable. In this second novel, Asimov was trying to impress by using fancy language. Brad asked him. "Do you know how Hemingway says, 'The sun rose the next morning?'"

"No," Asimov answered. "How does he say it?"

"He says, 'The sun rose the next morning.'"

The end of the decade of the 1940s included a lot of other endings. It was the end of the assistantship at Columbia, of Asimov's stay at Columbia itself, and—at least for now—of his life in New York City. It was also a time of some beginnings. He had sold a short story, a serial, and a book. He had gotten two stories anthologized. He had options on two more books. His writing life was on an upswing.

Once before, Asimov had tried to use an outline and failed. Now it happened again. He could not follow one. The story emerged as he worked, taking its own shape. He threw the outline away. After that, he refused to use an outline for anything he wrote.

As the new instructor began his teaching duties with freshmen, Isaac was quickly put in his place. At first, he felt very confident in his white lab coat with everyone calling him "Doctor." Then a student asked, "Pardon me, Dr. Asimov, are you a Ph.D. or a real doctor?" Even though he had earned his degree through rigorous original research, in the medical school the M.D. degree meant more than the Ph.D. degree.

As he got ready for his first lecture, he went to the professor in charge with a worry. "Last night I dreamed I got up before the class to give my lecture and I couldn't think of a thing to say. Do you think there's something ominous in that?"

"I think there's something normal in that," he said. "We all have dreams like that. Wait till you dream that you not only can't think of a thing to say but that you're standing there naked."

Isaac soon discovered that he disliked academic politics.

The cover of Isaac's first published novel, *Pebble in the Sky*.

A fellow instructor got promoted to assistant professor even though Asimov had been hired before him. The secret was that the instructor had his M.D.

Asimov labeled the year 1950 as the one in which he outgrew the editor John Campbell. Campbell had been his chief editor for almost twelve years. For that he was grateful. But in later years Campbell had gone in new directions. He became a follower of L. Ron Hubbard's philosophy, called dianetics, which later became the basis for Scientology. Campbell began demanding compliance with his views before he would publish a writer's work in *Astounding*. Asimov was not about to compromise his principles. Besides, new possibilities were on the horizon. Now was the time to stop relying on just one editor. Writing books was more satisfying and financially rewarding than writing short stories.

Other things were also highly satisfying and financially rewarding. Throughout their moves, the Asimovs had been hindered in their housing choices by the need for mass transit: neither one could drive, so they had to live near bus or train lines. Now that they could afford a car, they wanted to get their licenses. From the moment he got behind the wheel, Asimov loved driving. Soon he had his license, and their housing and traveling options opened up.

Gertrude wanted to know where Asimov got his writing ideas. "Anywhere," he answered on a drive back from New York. "I could write a story about a trip from Boston to New York, for instance." After some thought, he told her of a plot hatching in his mind at that moment. The next night he started the story, entitled "What If?—." He completed it in two weeks.

Whatever he was doing must have been working. In 1950 he earned $4700 at his writing alone. The combined income for the year was $10,000—nearly half of his income was from writing.

He would need the money. The couple had tried for years to have children and had finally given up. Then Gertrude discovered that she was pregnant. He was thirty-one years old, Gertrude thirty-three; they had been married nine years. They would need a roomier apartment. While they were hunting for one, Gertrude had some complications. Asimov panicked and took her directly to the hospital. Her doctor seemed unconcerned, but Asimov continued to worry. The joke going around among the nurses was "Gertrude did not have a miscarriage, but Isaac had five."

Asimov was becoming increasingly dissatisfied with his job. He wanted more positive feelings than he was getting from his university job. Dr. Lemon, his supervisor, became increasingly difficult to work for. Lemon lacked a sense of humor and was very serious about research and about the publicity it gained for the school. Asimov thought more and more about devoting full time to writing.

As time went on, things got somewhat better. The baby inside Gertrude was showing signs of life and seemed healthy. Asimov and Gertrude found a larger apartment. At work, although he didn't get a promotion, he got a raise.

The Asimovs went to classes for soon-to-be parents, where they learned about diaper changing and feeding. They also bought a stroller, some baby-bathing equipment, and a bed for the baby. They both enjoyed having something in common with friends who were raising families, instead of feeling wistful about not having children of their own.

One evening Gertrude began to have regular labor pains but didn't want to become overly alarmed. Asimov, on the other hand, was getting quite upset that he might have to deliver the baby on the way to the hospital.

They had a long wait. She was in the labor room fifteen hours. Finally the doctor came out and said, "Congratulations, Isaac. It's a boy." David Asimov was a premature baby. Because he was underweight, the baby stayed in the hospital one more day after Gertrude could leave.

David had an allergy to milk. His parents switched to a soymilk, which gave the nutrition without the dairy. Gradually the red spots he had developed went away.

Asimov became so disturbed about his lack of promotion at the university that he looked elsewhere for work. A nearby Veterans Administration Hospital had a job opening that was somewhat more attractive than his present position. He went to his superior, Dr. Walker, and said that if he did not get a professorship, he would take the offer of a job elsewhere. Walker agreed to an assistant professor status.

Gertrude and Asimov had to curtail their movie going, even though they were avid movie fans, because of their new son. In a way, this was unfortunate for Asimov. Movies were his escape. He enjoyed action/adventure films and comedies. He did not enjoy most science-fiction films because he found them poorly done. He rarely went to movies to be enlightened. Movies were his safety valve for daily pressures.

A solution was waiting—television. In 1952 they bought a set. At first they watched everything. After a while, however, they began to choose their favorites—mainly comedies. Asimov became very rigid about not missing his

Isaac with his son David at a science-fiction convention. (Photo by Jay Kay Klein)

favorite shows. Once he almost destroyed a friendship when he refused to accept a dinner invitation because it would interfere with a scheduled program.

Asimov was losing interest in research. The prospect of spending the rest of his life doing research seemed unbearable. Until he began writing nonfiction, he had easily been able to separate his research life from his writing life. But now that he wrote more nonfiction, he was beginning to see himself more as a writer than a researcher.

The climate at the Boston University medical school was worsening. A copy of a scholarly journal containing Asimov's review of some chemistry literature arrived. He shared it with his supervisor in an effort to show that he was keeping up in the field and publishing. Lemon's response was "Why don't you put this effort into your research?"

Asimov responded angrily, "I did this on my own time."

Lemon countered, "A research worker doesn't have his own time." Now Asimov knew that they did not see things the same way. He decided immediately that his days as a research chemist were ending.

This did not mean that he hated teaching. He was satisfied with that part of his work, and students seemed to be also. Sometimes in the middle of a lecture he gave very colorful descriptions about some aspect of the topic. Students laughed and applauded. One-on-one, he also tended to joke and act informally. Some other faculty members did not approve of the lighter, informal approach, feeling that Asimov was getting too friendly with students. But his style happened to be less formal, and it worked with the students.

Chapter Six

Family and Nonfiction

Asimov did not want the responsibility of buying a house, but he could afford it now, and they felt that it would be good for David. They began a long search. The first houses they looked at were either too expensive or too rundown.

His writing earnings in 1952 came to $8550—one and a half times his school earnings. This was the peak of science-fiction's popularity, with many new magazines being started every month. That was just as well, considering that Campbell's new interest, now that he was finished with dianetics, was parapsychology. He was becoming increasingly conservative and anti-science, and asked that stories reflect his interests.

David was learning about the world. When Asimov took him for walks, he always wanted to go the opposite way. He discovered TV knobs and loved to make the picture jump or roll. If his parents were watching a program and got angry, though, he quickly readjusted the set to their satisfaction.

In spite of his growing fame, Asimov could not get beyond rejections. He started a series of science-fiction novels for young readers called the Lucky Starr books. One the series was rejected. The short story "The Singing Bell" was sent back by both *Ellery Queen* and *Astounding*. Fred

Pohl, now working for Ballantine Books, rejected it as well. The magazine *Fantasy and Science Fiction* refused "It's Such a Beautiful Day."

Asimov was now an assistant professor but wanted a promotion to associate professor so that he could gain the security of tenure. By 1954, he felt he had gone as far as he could in both the university work and his science-fiction. It was time to seek new directions.

Gertrude was pregnant again. Now their house hunting became more urgent.

Asimov received his largest royalty check yet—$4400 from Doubleday. His writing earnings by September 1954 had stretched beyond $10,000, a feat he had once considered impossible. By the end of 1954, his writing earnings were twice what he made at the university.

February 19, 1955, Gertrude gave birth to a girl. They named her Robyn with the *y* so that it would have a different spelling from *Robin*, which could be either a boy or a girl. Asimov called her Robbie. When David was born, Asimov had moved his office into the master bedroom. After Robyn's birth, he moved into the hallway. The quarters were cramped but would have to do until they found a house.

Asimov received official notice that he had been promoted to associate professor. This meant that he had tenure and would not have to worry about loss of job. Or so he thought.

In their twelfth year together, Asimov and Gertrude were having marriage difficulties. During one of their trips to visit relatives in New York, Gertrude got angry with him. Taking care of the two small children and hunting for a house was making her bitter. As he drove the family home to Boston, Asimov wondered whether his marriage had failed. He

Isaac with Robyn when she was twelve-years-old. (Photo by Jay Kay Klein)

didn't think he had made Gertrude happy. He knew he lived only for his writing and didn't like to do the things other people enjoyed doing, such as traveling. He hadn't been able to find a decent house. Still, he could not change the way he was. The thought of divorce crossed his mind. It crossed her mind sometimes too. As time went on, unable to make her happy, he retreated into work even more.

Isaac realized he didn't fit the work world any better than the marriage world. Ever since graduate school, he had been less than enthusiastic about chemistry. He continued to be too loud and casual for the academic world. He was the same now as he had been when he worked in his father's candy store. Back then he had gotten into trouble when he forgot to greet the customers he met outside the store. Once again he was failing to show proper respect for authority.

The Asimovs finally bought a house in West Newton, a suburb of Boston about two miles south of their apartment. The main floor had a large living room/dining area, a kitchen, and three small bedrooms. The basement contained two large rooms that needed finishing—one a playroom, the other a laundry. A two-car heated garage was under the bedrooms. The backyard measured a quarter acre. Two finished attic rooms would serve as Asimov's office.

That March brought particularly bad winter weather. The wide driveway was handy; but with snow, shoveling became a major problem. When heat from inside melted snow on the roof, water went into the basement. In addition, the hot-water tank had to be replaced. Because the walkway was directly under the eaves, slick ice formed from water drips. In fall, leaves created a raking chore. Then there was the lawn mowing.

At a science-fiction convention, Isaac, in discomfort because of a kidney stone, was grumpy as he autographed books. Seeing him there, a woman dashed over to a bookseller and purchased an Asimov novel so she would have something he could sign. When the line got down to her, Isaac scowled and asked, "What's your name?"

"Janet Jeppson." She spelled it out.

"And what do you do?" he asked.

"I'm a psychiatrist," she answered.

"Good," he said, "let's get on the couch together."

Puzzled by this remark, she walked away with her copy of his signed novel. This was the first time Isaac met Janet, but not his last.

As he did more science writing, Asimov began to understand a difference between fiction and nonfiction. When he wrote fiction, each piece had to be different from the others. In nonfiction, however, a piece could be rewritten and submitted to various publications. When he wrote about blood types, for example, he might write one way for science educators, another way for a scholarly journal, a third way for a magazine selling to the general public, and a fourth for juveniles. Also, when it was rejected, it was just rejected, without the complicated instructions for revision that often accompanied fiction rejections. Then there were the financial advantages of nonfiction. He sold an article on appetite, obesity, and dieting for ten cents a word. This was more than double what he got for science-fiction. The major national publication *Mademoiselle* published the article, which meant that many more people saw it than saw his science-fiction stories. He devoted less time to writing fiction.

Chapter Seven

Full-time Writer

Isaac wanted reassurance that his publishing was moving along smoothly before he left his teaching job. He had sent a manuscript for a mystery novel called *Sit with Death* to Doubleday, but an editor told him they did not want it. This was the first outright rejection he had received from Doubleday. It made him doubt his ability to support his family as a writer.

The same day Doubleday rejected his mystery novel, the Soviet Union shot its satellite, Sputnik I, into space. Suddenly, there was an increased demand for science-fact writers and speakers.

Isaac went to a meeting with Keefer and Sinex, his superiors at the university. Keefer said that Asimov was to do more research, and not write on school time. Asimov refused that demand. Keefer answered, "This school cannot afford to pay a science writer. Your appointment will come to an end as of June 30, 1958."

"Very well, Dr. Keefer." Isaac shot back. "You may refuse to pay me a salary. In return, I will do no teaching for the school. However, there is no way you can take away my title. I have tenure."

Keefer claimed he did not have tenure. During the next two years, the two fought over this point. Asimov felt justified in battling for the prestige of the title. He remained confident during the struggle because he had an outside income. At the time he stopped teaching, Asimov was making five times more as a writer than as an associate professor.

Now Isaac was a full-time writer. During the first two years, he wrote mainly for teenagers. He believed they needed a sound introduction to science. He also enjoyed the informal style he could use in juvenile books. He remembered with distaste the adult textbooks he had written.

Asimov had been doing a science column for a magazine called *Venture* until it folded. Then the editor of *F&SF* (*Fantasy and Science Fiction*) asked him to continue the column with that magazine. Asimov was delighted. The columns began with a length of 1200 words, but soon expanded to 4000 words. At first, the editor tried to steer Asimov in certain ways, but he soon gave up and let Asimov do what he wanted. He began calling his new columnist "The Good Doctor." The articles helped Isaac develop his casual science-fact writing style.

Asimov was scheduled to attend the Mystery Writers of America convention. When he heard about the death of a good friend, he felt despondent and almost canceled. At the dinner he sat next to Janet Jeppson, the psychiatrist he had made the crude remark to at a previous autograph signing. He did not remember meeting her before. They chatted throughout dinner. During the after-dinner speech he held Janet's hand, and she didn't object. After the awards ceremony, the two spent the rest of the evening talking.

Besides attending conventions, he also became a public speaker. For some time, Asimov had enjoyed giving talks to groups even though he received no pay. Most of the speaking engagements were carried out with no preparation. A friend asked him to address the local PTA. To his surprise, Asimov received ten dollars for the talk. Asimov gave his second paid speech to Harvard University's undergraduate chemistry club. He earned fifteen dollars. In August 1959, he was invited to speak at Cornell University. He was offered five hundred dollars. At first he thought it must be a mistake. He found out that the offer was genuine.

In June 1959 Asimov took the family on a vacation trip to Provincetown, Rhode Island. The climb to the top of the Provincetown monument winded him but didn't bother the kids at all. At the top, he was afraid to look over the edge. The kids showed no fear. Trying to keep his fright hidden so they wouldn't develop it themselves, he forced his head over the railing and pretended to enjoy the view.

This two-day vacation was enjoyable. He learned that hastily planned, short vacations seemed better than carefully planned, long ones.

Isaac began to earn a reputation for being a prolific author. People thought he was a magician to write so much. When asked if he worked on more than one project at once. He answered, "Yes, I do, but only one thing at any one time."

"Do you switch from one to another?" one person asked.

"At will."

"What if you get writer's block?"

"I don't ever get one precisely because I switch from one task to another at will. If I'm tired of one project, I just switch to something else which interests me more."

Isaac said he never suffered from writer's block because he was always working on more than one project at a time. (Photo by Jay Kay Klein)

By 1960, Asimov had accumulated enough of his column articles from *F&SF* to collect into a book. He took the idea, along with a carefully selected batch of essays, to a Houghton Mifflin editor, who liked it and pursued it. Although Houghton Mifflin later rejected the manuscript, Asimov knew that someone would want it. Doubleday took it.

Asimov began to wonder whether he might publish one hundred books before he died. When he approached his wife with the idea, she answered, "Maybe you can reach your goal, Isaac, but what good will it be if you then regret having spent your time writing books while all the essence of life passes you by?"

He explained, "But for me, the essence of life *is* writing. In fact, if I do manage to publish a hundred books, and if I then die, my last words are likely to be, 'Only a hundred!'"

Rejections still happened. The New York *Times Sunday Magazine* wanted him to write an article about science-fiction conventions. When he sent in a comic version, the editor refused it. Later, the editor accepted a more serious version. After that, when that editor requested articles, he rejected them as often as he accepted them. A *Playboy* editor asked Asimov to write a story based on an illustration, but rejected three attempts in a row.

January 6, 1961, Asimov received an advance copy of his book *Words from the Myths*. It was his forty-sixth book, and he got this copy on his fifty-first birthday. In November 1961 he received a royalty check from Doubleday for $27,600. It was five times larger than any previous check. His 1961 income came to just over $69,000, fourteen times what he had made as a Boston University professor. While this was pleasing, it was bittersweet. He had reached a height he felt he could not surpass. He didn't want to spend the next thirty years in a decline.

Asimov found out that the more books and articles he published, the more other publishers and magazines wanted him for new projects. Because he knew what it felt like to get rejected, he did not want to reject requests from others. He often found himself working on too many tasks and then resenting his obligation to complete them.

Even though he was taking on more than he could handle, even with his highly disciplined work schedule, he could not resist taking on new projects. He became skillful at suggesting sequels to editors. As soon as Doubleday accepted the *F&SF* essay collection, he planned to suggest a second set of them. As soon as Houghton Mifflin accepted *Words from Genesis*, Asimov was ready to move with words from other books of the Bible.

Asimov was very content with his full-time publishing life. Nevertheless, there were times when he was bothered that he had turned his back on doing scientific research. He felt better when he found a notable scientist who enjoyed his works. One time, at dinner with a famous computer researcher, Asimov was delighted to learn that the man regularly read his articles in *F&SF*. He was also happy when he found out that his writing had influenced research. A young university physicist wrote that reading one of Asimov's essays had changed the research he was doing. In a way, Asimov felt he was still contributing to research even though he had left it.

Asimov's classic science-fiction short story "Nightfall," and his highly respected *Intelligent Man's Guide to Science* moved him toward fame in their separate fields. Figures coming in on his book-length science-fiction established that he was a moneymaker. His Foundation stories, which had been gathered together into three volumes—*Foundation, Foundation and Empire,* and *Second Foundation*—and *I, Robot,* a collection of his robot stories, brought in more money than his other books.

Isaac worked a year and a half on a book of science biographies. It was three or four times as long as he had originally planned. On March 28, 1963, he took ten boxes of manuscripts to his editor's office. He put six into plain view; the rest, copies of the originals, he hid under a desk. Then he went to get his editor. Seeing the six boxes, Tom Seldes was shocked. But he decided to take things in stride. "Which of these boxes are the original and which the carbon?" he asked.

"They're all original, Tom," Asimov answered. He revealed the other four boxes and added, "These are the carbons." This huge manuscript became *Asimov's Biographical Encyclopedia of Science and Technology,* the first book to have his name in the title.

Isaac received science-fiction's highest honor, the Hugo Award, at the 1963 World Science Fiction Convention, "for putting the science in science-fiction." He was being recognized for his essays in *F & SF.*

TV Guide asked Asimov to do a commentary on a new program about a robot called "My Living Doll." He wrote a humorous piece entitled "How Not to Build a Robot," which was successful. In future years the magazine asked for other articles.

World Book, the encyclopedia publisher, hired Asimov as the science writer on its team to create a Yearbook. The company planned for its next meeting to be in Bermuda. Because he feared flying, Asimov decided he would not go. When the invitation came, he replied that he would not attend. An angry letter came back, threatening to fire him from the project if he did not attend. Isaac still refused to go. After one more article for World Book, the editors replaced him with another scientist.

The head of special collections at Boston University began collecting all of Isaac's papers and books for its archives and wanted asked for his help. He put together what he had and took them to the library. When the department head asked what had happened to the rest, he answered, "Lately, I've been giving some of the stuff to the Newton Public Library, but mostly I've been burning them. You know, when they crowd up my filing cabinets, and I don't need them anymore, I get rid of them. They're just junk." He then received a lecture on the importance of saving everything for the sake of research. Asimov was so touched that he promised to be better about saving things.

The World Science Fiction Convention organizers created a special category called "Best All-time Novel Series" to be eligible for a Hugo. Asimov knew that his Foundation series, which had been nominated, was popular, but thought he had little chance of winning the award. J.R.R. Tolkien's Lord of the Rings triology, then highly popular, had also been nominated, along with Heinlein's Future History series, Isaac's boyhood favorite E.E. Smith's Lensmans series, and Edgar Rice Burroughs' Mars series. When the announcer opened the envelope and read "Isaac Asimov for the Foundation series," Isaac thought it was a practical joke. He just sat there until everyone began laughing. Then it dawned on him that he had really won the award. He knew now that his Foundation series was a science-fiction classic.

The October 1966 issue of *F&SF* was devoted to Isaac Asimov. It contained a short story and a poem by him, as well as a partial bibliography of his works. Also in that issue was his 96th *F&SF* essay, entitled "Portrait of the Writer as a Boy," which told about his beginnings as a writer.

Asimov was contacted to do a novel based on the movie *Fantastic Voyage*. After reading the screenplay, he agreed on the condition that he could make the ending more realistic. He revised an earlier books for young people called *Inside the Atom*. The Atomic Energy Commission wanted him to write some pamphlets on the effects of radiation. The magazine *Science Digest* encouraged his gradual takeover of its column "Please Explain," which in time became "Isaac Asimov Explains." He did research for a book on the Roman civilization.

Now that a history book he had written called *The Greeks* seemed to be doing well, Asimov visited his editor. "Does this mean that I can start work on the Romans now if I want to?" he asked.

"Yes, you can begin any time."

"And bring it in whenever I'm finished?"

"Whenever you're finished."

"Good." Asimov pulled his briefcase nearer. "I've just finished it. Here it is!"

Besides dealing with editors, he took care of work normally done by writers' agents. Early in his career, Asimov had found that he could represent himself better than a paid agent could. One job an agent usually performed was copyright renewals. After twenty-eight years, copyrights had to be renewed or given up. "Marooned Off Vesta," first published in 1938, was coming up for renewal. Asimov filed the renewal request, then checked on other renewal dates coming up. From then on, he knew he would have to deal with copyright renewals. Now he knew that he had attained his childhood goal of writing for a living.

Chapter Eight

Fame and Fortune

By the middle of the 1960s, Asimov had been concentrating on nonfiction for a decade. There had developed a new generation of science-fiction writers, such as Robert Silverberg and Philip K. Dick, who wrote stories that were bolder and more wildly imaginative than most of Isaac's work. Isaac had early in his career developed a clear and simple style to write his novels about robots and time travel and the rise and fall of galactic empires. It had served him well because his work was, for the most part, in the tradition of "hard science-fiction." This meant that the scientific ideas in his stories were at least theoretically possible, and were based on current understandings of science.

As Isaac considered returning to science-fiction, he feared that the field had passed him by. He thought his ideas were old fashioned and his style too plain to appeal to the new generation of science-fiction readers. When his friend Evelyn del Rey, the wife of Lester del Rey, asked "Why don't you write science-fiction these days, Isaac?" he said, "Evelyn, you know as well as I do that the field has moved beyond me."

She responded, "Isaac, you're crazy. When you write, you *are* the field." He needed that encouragement. When he decided to try science-fiction again, her words helped him to succeed.

As Isaac's fame grew, TV appearances became more frequent. He taped an episode of "The Twenty-first Century" with Walter Cronkite. Before the interview began, Asimov wanted to say to him, "My father will be very thrilled, Mr. Cronkite, when he finds out you've interviewed me." But he felt that would sound immature and said nothing.

During a pause in the taping, Mr. Cronkite said, "Well, Dr. Asimov, my father will be very thrilled when he finds out I've interviewed you."

Ever since the Asimovs had moved to their Newton home, they had experienced trouble with passing teenagers who loitered and trespassed on the grass. Gertrude had some shouting matches with the kids, to no avail. One day, feeling cheerful after some good news on the phone from an editor, Asimov went out and told Gertrude to go inside; he would handle the problem. He spent time with the kids, kidding and joking. He told them how many books he had published and explained that he needed quiet to write. The teenagers became cooperative. Asimov could not understand why his wife and he had never tried this approach before.

The Asimov children were now teenagers. David was more frequently requesting use of the family car. Robyn was increasing her use of the family phone. At last the situation became bad enough that a second phone had to be installed. Asimov could not afford to have his business interrupted.

While Gertrude and Robyn were vacationing in Europe, the Sunday New York *Times* published an interview with Asimov that had been conducted the previous April. At the end of the interview was a tribute to Asimov's father for purchasing a typewriter even though young Isaac had not gotten anything published yet. Asimov called his parents in Florida, where they had moved a few months earlier, to find out if they had seen the article. His mother said that his father wasn't feeling well. The father got on the phone and said she was exaggerating. He promised to read the *Times* article. Later in the day, his father called Asimov back and said how pleased he was with the article.

The day after his phone call about the *Times* article, Asimov got an emergency call from his brother Stan in New York. Their father had died that afternoon. He was seventy-two years old and had lived with a heart problem for thirty-one years. Asimov was glad his father had seen the *Times* article before he died.

After the funeral, with his wife and daughter in Europe, and David away at a private school, Isaac felt lonely. He worked hard on a Shakespeare book, but nights were difficult. He was grieving with no one to console him. The pain of his kidney stone returned. Then Janet Jeppson, who was vacationing in New England, called him. He suggested lunch. After lunch, they toured Concord and other historical sites. She thoroughly enjoyed the afternoon, and her joy lessened his pain. After dinner that night, they agreed to spend the next day sightseeing. When he picked her up the next morning, they went to Salem and Marblehead. Asimov felt the two days helped alleviate both the pain of his father's death and his kidney stone ailment.

Later, while sitting beside an attractive British movie actress during the taping of a "Dick Cavett Show," Isaac made flirtatious remarks to her that Gertrude did not like.

She let him know how displeased she was over his behavior. From that point on, their marriage moved toward divorce. Shortly after the TV broadcast, Gertrude visited her mother in New York and stayed several days. During that time, Asimov had his lawyer write her a letter suggesting that they follow through with their much-discussed divorce.

In his autobiography, Asimov reflected: "I don't suppose marriages turn sour in a moment. You don't fall off a precipice. It's just that annoyances multiply, frictions come slowly to seem irreconcilable, forgiveness comes more reluctantly and with worse grace. And then, one day, you're shaking your head with the knowledge that the marriage isn't working."

In June, 1970 Isaac and Gertrude separated after twenty-eight years of marriage. With Janet Jeppson's help, he found an apartment in New York. The first work he completed in his new bachelor apartment was *Isaac Asimov's Treasury of Humor*. Eventually, he spent most of his non-working hours at Janet's place.

Isaac worried that this life-style change might affect his writing productivity. However, the New York move proved more stimulating to his writing, not less. For one thing, most publishers were located nearby. But also, the artistic atmosphere of New York motivated him.

That year, he spent Thanksgiving with Janet's family. He was made to feel right at home. He even accomplished something no one else had ever done—got the pet terrier to bark. When he moved to the floor to watch a TV program with one of Janet's younger relatives, the dog became protective and let out its first bark ever. Once he discovered the noise, the dog didn't want to stop making it.

On July 11, 1971, John Campbell died. This was nearly as shocking to Asimov as his father's death had been. After all, Campbell had been his literary father. At the memorial service, Asimov read the Twenty-third Psalm. Back at the Campbell house, Campbell's wife insisted on no sadness.

Asimov's mother had moved back north to a Long Island retirement home after his father's death in Florida. Asimov was saddened to see his mother's health worsen. She suffered from congestive heart failure and had to go to the hospital from time to time. He noticed that she was growing feebler and more helpless.

Approached to do a short-story collection called *The Early Asimov*, Asimov at first refused. He felt that some inferior stories should not go to press. Later, he realized that for the sake of historical record and objective research, the public should see them. He changed his mind and agreed to the book.

Now that Asimov was spending more time with Janet, who was a physician, she worried over his health. She convinced him to visit a competent internist for a physical checkup and accompanied him to make sure he got there. The doctor found a thyroid nodule, a slight swelling on the side of his neck.

The thyroid problem would need attention. Asimov grew increasingly worried over the prospect of having his thyroid removed. He turned to his brother Stanley for encouragement. Stan had earlier undergone surgery for a slipped disc. As he usually did in times of stress, Isaac kept himself busy, this time working on *Asimov's Biographical Encyclopedia of War and Battle*. Even so, evenings were lonely. His main concern was that he might not get to finish his work if he

Isaac and his second wife, Janet. (Photo by Jay Kay Klein)

died. But then he remembered that he had published 117 books to date. Thus, as he stated in his autobiography, ". . . I had made my peace with death." He was able to face surgery in a cheerful mood.

As the nurses prepared his for surgery by sedating him, Isaac became less inhibited. Being wheeled through the hall on a gurney, he sang a baritone aria from a favorite opera. Once he got to the operating room, he called the surgeon over and confided:

> Doctor, doctor, in your green coat,
> Doctor, doctor, cut my throat.
> And when you've finished, doctor, then,
> Won't you sew it up again.

The surgeon was so overwhelmed with laughter that he had trouble controlling his cutting hand. After the operation, he asked Isaac why he had had the poor judgment to make an operating surgeon laugh. Asimov knew the answer: he would do anything for a laugh.

Nineteen months after Asimov had moved back to New York, he became legally separated. It would be another year before he could qualify for a divorce.

Janet went to the hospital for exploratory surgery on her breast. Isaac expected the operation to be finished by 5:00 p.m. At 6:00 she still was not out of the operating room, and he was panic-stricken. Finally, the surgeon informed him that they had removed the left breast. When Asimov visited her in the recovery room, she was still groggy but managed to say, "I'm sorry."

Visiting Janet the next day, he found her depressed and worried about how she would look. He tried to console her, but she wouldn't listen. Finally, he took another approach.

He stood up, shook a finger, and said, "Listen! What's all this fuss about? If you were a showgirl, I could see where taking off the left breast would be tragic. You would be all unbalanced, and you would fall over to the right side. In your case, with your tiny breasts, who cares? In a year, I'll be looking at you and squinting my eyes and saying, 'Which breast did the surgeon remove?'" That did it. She laughed. From that time on, his approach in dealing with her feelings about the breast removal was to use humor.

The day after Janet returned home from the hospital, Robyn arrived. She had not yet met Janet. Isaac was afraid they would not get along, but everything went fine. He took Robyn to a performance of Shakespeare in the Park, which she enjoyed thoroughly. Soon Robyn left for Wyndham College in Putney, Vermont.

In Boston on business, Asimov called Janet to let her know that he had arrived safely. On the phone, she acted confused and said she had been sleeping. But she had trouble understanding what he was talking about. She also was very forgetful. Later in the day he got a call from a relative of Janet, who said Janet was in the hospital. A patient had arrived at her office for an appointment. When she discovered that Janet was not well, she called a doctor, who came right over and then called an ambulance.

Back in New York at the hospital, Asimov found that she was in intensive care because doctors suspected a stroke. Later, they found that bleeding had taken place in the outer area of the brain, not inside it, and that the cause of bleeding was rupture of a blood vessel so small that she would have little difficulty recovering.

Not long after Janet's hospitalization, there was a phone

call from Asimov's sister: his mother had died peacefully in her sleep at the Long Island hotel where she lived. Isaac and Janet went to Long Island so that he could identify the body. His mother had died four years and two days after his father, one month before her seventy-eighth birthday.

Through this sad time, Isaac kept busy with his writing. He finished a book called *Eyes on the Universe,* and writing another of his mystery stories for a popular series called "The Black Widower."

Editors at Ginn and Company had a problem with a science-text series Asimov was working on. Conservative school systems were not adopting the texts because of Asimov's treatment of evolution. They wanted the word "development" to replace "evolution." Furious, Asimov refused to go along with the change. He said that if they removed the term, they would have to also remove his name. The term "evolution" stayed until another writer took over the series.

On September 16, 1973, Asimov's divorce became official, twenty-one months after his separation from Gertrude, three and a half years after he had left Newton, thirty-one years after his marriage. His legal fees amounted to $50,000.

Now that the divorce was official, Asimov could think of remarriage. He and Janet arranged to be married in her apartment. Because they were not religious, an official from the Ethical Culture movement performed the ceremony. The night before the wedding, Asimov found Janet crying. She said, "I feel as though I'll be losing my identity."

Isaac said, "Don't look upon it as losing identity; look upon it as gaining subservience," and she turned from crying to laughter.

Chapter Nine

Returning Home to Science Fiction

Over the years, Isaac had received a large number of rejections from the New York *Times*. He hoped to someday get an opportunity to turn down a request from them to write an article. When he finally got a call from a New York *Times* editor, he prepared to refuse his offer. However, they wanted a science-fiction story, which was a highly unusual request from such a prominent newspaper. It was a challenge he couldn't resist.

Once Isaac was traveling by taxi through the New York streets after an interview at a TV station. The driver asked what he had been doing in the station. Asimov said, "Being interviewed."

"You an actor?" the driver wondered.

"No. I'm a writer."

"I once wanted to be a writer," the driver reminisced, "but I never got around to it."

"Just as well," Asimov observed. "You can't make a living as a writer."

The cabbie disagreed: "Isaac Asimov does."

Asimov didn't know how to answer.

The country's view of science-fiction had changed over the years. The genre seemed to be entering the mainstream of life as well as of literature. Frequently the name Asimov got connected with the idea of science-fiction, even though most of his later work had been in the field of nonfiction. An example was the appearance of Asimov's science-fiction piece "The Life and Times of Multivac" in the New York *Times*. In the same issue was an article on triage, the decision-making process used during medical emergencies to decide who would be allowed to die and who of the injured will be saved. The editor of a medical journal, seeing both Asimov's name and the triage article, contacted the writer to do a story about triage. Asimov wrote the story for the journal, and it was published. *High Fidelity* magazine wanted a story on sound. *Bell Telephone* magazine requested one on communications. Asimov was happy.

Asimov taped three segments for the "Today" show with Barbara Walters. Off-camera, Barbara kept trying to get him to talk about what he did—or would like to do—besides write. He continued to answer that he really did not care to do anything but write. Finally she put it this way: "What if the doctors told you that you only had six months to live. What would you do then?"

Asimov answered, "Type faster."

He finished the first draft of his novel *Murder at the ABA*, a book suggested by Larry Ashmead, a Doubleday editor. Earlier, a European had written a mystery called *The Frankfurt Murder*, which took place at a book fair in Germany. Larry had latched on to this idea and suggested it to Asimov. After writing many mystery short stories, Asimov thought he might be ready for a full-length work. The suggestion came at the end of May 1975, when the American Book Association would be holding its book fair in New York City. Larry suggested that Asimov attend the fair to get ideas. After the convention, he asked Asimov, "Do you think you can write a mystery based on the convention?"

Asimov answered, " I think so. I already have a plot ready."

"Good," Larry nudged. "We'll need it in time for the next convention."

"You'll have the manuscript in your hands long before next Memorial Day."

"Not the manuscript, Isaac. The complete book!" It turned out that he had two months to go from idea through finished manuscript.

He considered Larry one of his best editors. He had a degree in geology and was very helpful editing the science books. They often had lunch together. Larry had a keen sense of humor. One time he talked Asimov into having a second dessert, promising he would not tell Janet. When Asimov got home, Janet met him at the door, saying, "What is this about two desserts?" The practical joker had been at work.

While in Boston to give a speech, Asimov wanted to take his daughter out to dinner. She asked if she could bring a friend. The friend turned out to be five friends. On their way to the expensive restaurant, Asimov joked, "Girls, feeding you all is going to be expensive, so I hope you will confine yourselves to mixed green salads and, perhaps, grapefruit for dessert." Robyn was worried that they wouldn't understand his sense of humor, but they laughed and ate big meals.

Science-fiction was changing. "Star Trek" conventions had become extremely popular. At one of them, Asimov served on a panel discussing the status of science-fiction. Several of the panelists were becoming weary of science-fiction and were trying to move away from it. They wanted to call their work "speculative fiction." Asimov insisted that he liked science-fiction as a field, and he liked the term.

A new venture appeared on the horizon—Asimov's own science-fiction magazine. Joel Davis, publisher of the *Ellery Queen's Mystery Magazine*, suggested a science-fiction periodical with Asimov's name in the title. They would find an editor to work with Isaac so that he wouldn't be stuck doing all the detail work. Asimov agreed to think about it, but secretly he hoped the project would disappear. It didn't. Joel Davis kept working until Isaac suggested that he hire George Scithers as the editor. The magazine was going to become a reality.

The president of Boston University sent him the following letter:

Dear Dr. Asimov,

In the course of flying to Chicago on American Airlines recently, I read with pleasure and profit your interesting article in the March 1976 issue of *American Way*. I took some pride in thinking that you maintain a continuing relationship as an Associate Professor of Biochemistry at the Boston University School of Medicine.

I wonder if I might ask you to assist me in communicating to the public the quality and stature of our School of Medicine and our University by indicating, when it is appropriate, your affiliation with Boston University. You will appreciate that the reputation of an institution is only as good as the reputation of its faculty and the student body. I believe that your many loyal readers might find it instructive to know of your relationship with the University.

Your help will be greatly appreciated.

/s/ John R. Silber

Asimov was struck by the contrast between this letter and the way he had been treated by Dr. Keefer eighteen years before. He wrote back and agreed to cooperate in letting others know about his former employer.

Walking through a dark auditorium in Syracuse, New York during one of their many speaking tours, Janet stumbled over some steps, injuring a foot. She suffered a hairline fracture and had to use crutches. Moving on to another speaking engagement in Jamestown, New York, south of Buffalo, they encountered further problems. Isaac came down with chills. He didn't know they were caused by a reaction to a sulfa drug he was taking. Since Janet already had her foot problem, he didn't mention his chills and kept taking the sulfa drug. By they time they arrived at Cornell University for another talk, he had a high fever. Because Janet couldn't drive, he had to. The Cornell schedule was very hectic. By the time they got back to New York, he barely had enough strength to climb into bed. Once doctors had him in the hospital, they changed his drug and he got better.

Janet's mother had been diagnosed with cancer. June 10, 1976, five months before her eightieth birthday, she died at home with Janet by her bedside. After her mother's death, Janet had to help empty the Westchester County house of its contents and sell it. The couple could have moved into the house, but both Janet and Asimov had grown used to city living and did not want to give up their apartment.

The first issue of *Isaac Asimov's Science Fiction Magazine* came out December 16, 1976. This first issue contained two stories by a well-known science-fiction writer of the time and a portion of a novel by another big name. It also included a review by the publisher of another science-fiction magazine, Asimov's editorial, and his short story entitled "Think!"

Cathleen Jordan, now Asimov's editor at Doubleday, was pressuring him to return to science-fiction. Instead, he suggested an autobiography and they agreed. After fifty pages, Asimov found that he was still only three years old. At this rate, the book promised to be very long. He wondered if Doubleday would want such a long autobiography. The blossoming of this book surprised Asimov: he had always assumed that his quiet life would not be much to write about. Two things worked in his favor. One was his highly retentive memory; the other was his diary he had kept since age eighteen.

Isaac slowly began returning to science-fiction. 1976 was the two hundreth anniversary of the Declaration of Independence and the entire country was celebrating. Isaac decided to do a short science-fiction novel in the spirit of the festivities. At a science-fiction banquet on April 30, 1976, Asimov did what he considered his best job of toastmastering ever. He also received a Nebula for "The Bicentennial Man," as best novelette of the year. Looking at the plaque, he found that his name had been misspelled "Issac Asmimov." Science Fiction Writers of America offered to fix the mistake, but he wanted it left that way as a conversation piece.

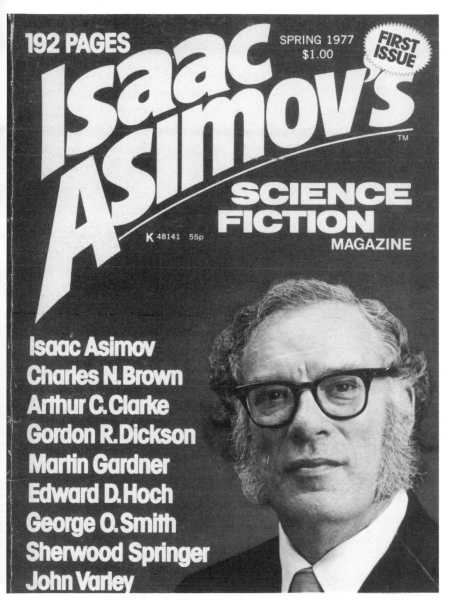

192 PAGES

SPRING 1977
$1.00

FIRST ISSUE

Isaac Asimov's

K 48141 55p

SCIENCE FICTION
MAGAZINE

™

Isaac Asimov
Charles N. Brown
Arthur C. Clarke
Gordon R. Dickson
Martin Gardner
Edward D. Hoch
George O. Smith
Sherwood Springer
John Varley

The cover of the first issue of *Isaac Asimov's Science Fiction Magazine.*

On an errand May 9, 1977, Asimov felt short of breath. He thought it could be an attack of angina pectoris, the same trouble his father had experienced. He now understood why during the past half year he had felt tired. Under pressure to complete several projects, including speaking engagements, Asimov decided to simply put up with the discomfort and watch what happened. One evening a cramp arrived which would not go away. Janet called their doctor, who took an electrocardiogram the next day. It came out normal, but Asimov knew he would have to lose weight. On another evening, when he experienced extreme pain, Asimov lectured Janet about how she should live her life if anything happened to him.

Scheduled for a doctor's appointment about a mile away from where he had attended a meeting, Asimov decided to test his angina: he walked to the building, then ran up the fourteen flights of stairs. This electrocardiogram revealed that Asimov had sometime previously suffered a mild coronary. Doctors immediately ordered him into the hospital. He had to postpone all speaking engagements. Once he was moved to a private room, Janet took him his draft of the autobiography so that he could revise it. Even while he was in the hospital, he got another project to work on—an article for *TV Guide*.

When the science-fiction writer Ben Bova visited Asimov in the hospital, he saw the sheets of paper from the autobiography manuscript all over the bed and asked what he was doing.

"In this autobiography," Asimov explained, "I'm including every stupid thing I can remember having said or done."

"Oh?" Bova said. "No wonder it's so long."

Once Asimov got home, he had to stay inside for the next two weeks. June 23, 1977, his doctor said he could resume normal working activity. He had recovered in time to see Robyn fly off on an eight-week trip to Europe. Meanwhile, his work kept coming out. July 26, the August 1977 issue of *Reader's Digest* hit the newsstands, containing an interview with him entitled "Asimov, the Human Writing Machine" and his essay for *Time* on low-energy use. By August, his autobiography had grown to 500,000 words and was in final form, ready for the editors.

Two events marked the end of 1977. One was his completion of the autobiography; the other was his being granted a full professorship by Boston University. He had only two regrets as he got on in years. One was that he had never learned the Russian language. If his parents had spoken Russian at home when he was a child, he would have become bilingual. The other was that there had not been enough money for him to learn piano. Even so, he knew that to keep up with either the language or the music, he would have had to use the skills continually. On the other hand, he felt that writing could be abandoned temporarily, then picked up again with no loss of skill.

Mortality was creeping up on Asimov. He had suffered the heart attack in 1977, at age fifty-seven. His hair was turning grey, his sideburns white. In 1978 his new eyeglasses had to have bifocals.

Other changes were on the horizon. Doubleday still wanted him to write a novel. Not just a novel, however—a science-fiction novel. And not just a science-fiction novel—a Foundation novel. This stunned Asimov: he hadn't written a Foundation story for thirty-two years. He was worried that he would fail at the task. He became doubly worried when Doubleday arranged for a $50,000 advance—half to be paid immediately, the other half upon completion of the manuscript.

His first job was to reread the *Foundation Trilogy.* When he finished reading, he understood what his readers had complained about. He too was bothered that there was not a fourth novel to enjoy. Now he wanted to write. The completion took nine months, and Foundation fans were waiting for the book to come off the presses. The week it came out, the book placed twelfth on the New York *Times* best-seller list. *Forward the Foundation* soon moved into third place and never left the list for twenty-five weeks. Asimov's income promptly doubled.

In the six years after his heart attack, Asimov published ninety books, two of them best-sellers. He refused to slow down. His chest pains and shortness of breath got steadily worse until he could barely function. Finally he admitted to his doctor that he was having difficulty breathing. On December 12, 1983, he entered the hospital for a heart bypass operation. His major fear was that his brain would be deprived of oxygen and he would suffer brain damage. He asked his personal physician to make sure his brain got plenty of oxygen. When the operation was over, the doctor, a personal friend, stopped in at the recovery room to check on Asimov's brain. He got Asimov's attention as he was coming out of the anesthesia and said, "Make me up a limerick, Isaac."

Asimov, slurred, "There once was an old doctor named Paul/ with a penis exceedingly small. . . ."

The doctor said, "That's enough, Isaac. You pass."

Isaac posing with the first editions of his published books. (Photo by Jay Kay Klein)

By the time he was sixty-seven, Asimov had won Hugo and Nebula awards and had published the best-selling books. He was one of the top science-fiction writers in America. In 1975, the Science Fiction Writers of America created a special Nebula called the Grand Master award. It was an award for someone's life work, and Asimov had always hoped he could get it. On May 2, 1987, he received it at the awards banquet.

In a 1989, at age 69, Asimov began to suffer from weariness, and his legs were not as cooperative as they had been. Fluid retention made his ankles puffy. In fact, his kidneys had been damaged by the heart-lung machine during bypass surgery. He changed to a salt-free diet and began taking diuretics.

His doctor detected a heart murmur and set up a round of tests. Dejected, Asimov cried and asked the doctor to let him die now that he had reached seventy. The doctor had him hospitalized immediately and put on an intravenous diuretic. He seemed to get better. But a heart valve had sprung a leak. Doctors did not advise surgery. On March 3, 1990, Asimov went home with a leaky valve and bad kidneys.

Asimov finished typing the last draft of his memoir *I. Asimov* May 30, 1990. The next day he went to Washington, D.C., where he met the Soviet leader Gorbachev at a luncheon. He continued to write every day. January 2, 1992, he wrote in his diary, "I made it. I'm seventy-one today. . . I got a birthday greeting in the 'Garfield' cartoon which probably gave me more exposure than I've ever had before! Robyn came and we went to Shun Lee for Peking duck and venison. It was great."

When typing became difficult, he dictated to Janet. In his farewell piece for *F&SF,* he said, "It has always been my ambition to die in harness with my head face down on a keyboard and my nose caught between two of the keys, but that's not the way it worked out."

Toward the end of his life, lying in bed at home, he slept a good share of the time. Once he woke and said to Janet, "I want . . . I want . . ."

"What is it, Isaac?" Janet asked.

"I want . . . I want . . ."

"What do you want, darling?"

"I want—Isaac Asimov!"

"Yes, that's you."

"I AM Isaac Asimov!"

"And Isaac Asimov can rest now."

"He smiled, said, "Okay," and went back to sleep.

On a visit to Asimov in the hospital, Janet said to him, "Isaac, you're the best there is." Isaac smiled, then shrugged. He raised his eyebrows and nodded yes.

He died on April 6, 1992, at age 72, of kidney failure. His last complete sentence to Janet and Robyn, as they held his hands, was "I love you too."

After his death, Janet found a scrap of paper on which he'd written:

> Over a space of 40 years, I sold an item every ten days on the average. Over the space of the second 20 years, I sold an item every six days on the average. Over a space of 40 years, I published an average of 1,000 words a day. Over the space of the second 20 years, I published an average of 1,700 words a day.

Toward the end of his memoir, Asimov gave this view of death:

> ... it is my opinion that we all achieve Nirvana at once, at the moment of the death that ends a single life. Since I have had a good life, I'll accept death as cheerfully as I can when it comes, although I would be glad to have that death painless. I would also be glad to have my survivors—relatives, friends, and readers—refrain from wasting their time and poisoning their lives in useless mourning and unhappiness. They should be happy instead, on my behalf, that my life has been so good.

Chapter Ten

Asimov's Legacy: A Reading Feast

Isaac Asimov once gave a talk to a group of librarians. There was the usual question session at the end. One of the audience members stood and said that Asimov had an honor. He was the author whose books got stolen most often from her library.

The stealing record may have occurred because he produced many books that appealed to a great variety of people. In his lifetime he wrote or edited over four hundred books. Few were specialty books for professionals. Most were for general readers.

The problem of selection becomes where to begin. If a reader starts searching in order of Asimov's writing phases, his first phase was science-fiction short stories. Most of those early pieces for the pulp fiction magazines have been assembled into collections. You might look for the following titles:

I, Robot (1950)—his robot stories connected with a running narrative—and *The Rest of the Robots* (1964)—more collected robot stories.

Nightfall and Other Stories (1969) includes the award-winning story that launched him into science-fiction fame.

Short story collections are *The Martian Way and Other*

Stories (1955), *The Early Asimov* (1972) (including stories he was not always proud of but that were a part of his writing past) *The Best of Isaac Asimov* (1973), *The Bicentennial Man and Other Stories* (1976) (includes the title story that Asimov cherished as one of his best works) *The Winds of Change and Other Stories* (1983).

The Complete Robot (1982) is a combination of the two robot volumes listed above plus previously unpublished stories

Robots and Empire (1985) attempts to link robots with his Foundation Series.

His first novel, *A Pebble in the Sky* (1950), explored the theme of prejudice and pitted individual will against society's will. *The Currents of Space* (1952) dealt with the idea of will as power and explored how the ends might justify the means. Asimov considered *The Caves of Steel* (1954) a model for much of his later novel writing. Many critics consider *The Gods Themselves* (1972) his best novel. *The Robots of Dawn* (1983) was a science-fiction mystery featuring a robot detective. *Nightfall* (1990) was an extension of the earlier short story into a book-length work. It was a collaboration with Robert Silverberg.

Asimov considered his 1958 short story "The Ugly Little Boy," one of his best. When his daughter Robyn read it, she broke down in tears. Every time Asimov himself read it, he cried. He and Robert Silverberg again collaborated to extend the story into a novel by the same name.

The Foundation Series earned him an award for best science-fiction series. While the books do not have to be read in order, many readers prefer to enjoy them that way. The first three books are known as the Foundation Trilogy.

These originally appeared as stories in the pulp fiction magazine *Astounding Science Fiction* between 1942 and 1949. They are *Foundation* (1951), *Foundation and Empire* (1952), and *Second Foundation* (1953). A fourth book added to the original trilogy, *Forward the Foundation* (1993), provided what fans had been wanting for many years a continuation promised in *Second Foundation*. Two other books were *Foundation's Edge* (1982) and *Foundation and Earth* (1986). The next to last volume, *Prelude to Foundation* (1988), came about after a discussion with a fan. The young person wanted to know more about the origin of Hari Seldon, the main character of the series. He wanted information that came before the first volume. Asimov thought this was such a good idea that he created this background for the series.

The prolific author gained his fame through science-fiction. He maintained it by becoming a science-fact writer. You can find books by him in the fields of general science, math, astronomy, earth science, chemistry, physics, and biology. He also compiled several scientific essay collections.

But he didn't stop there. He wrote for average readers about classical history and the Bible. If you are interested in these areas, read *The Greeks* (1965), *The Roman Republic* (1966), *The Roman Empire* (1967), *Asimov's Guide to the Bible, Volume I* (1968), and *Asimov's Guide to the Bible, Volume II* (1969). He also wrote *Asimov's Guide to Shakespeare* in 1970.

You can learn more about Asimov's life by reading his three autobiographies—*In Memory Yet Green* (1979), *In Joy Still Felt* (1980), and *I. Asimov* (1994).

Asimov's Books for Young People

Fiction

David Starr, Space Ranger New American Library, 1952
Lucky Starr and the Pirates of the Asteroids Fawcett Books, 1953
Lucky Starr and the Oceans of Venus Fawcett Crest, 1954
Lucky Starr and the Big Sun of Mercury Fawcett Crest, 1956
Lucky Starr and the Moons of Jupiter New American Library, 1957
Lucky Starr and the Rings of Saturn Fawcett Books, 1958
Norby, the Mixed-up Robot (with Janet Asimov) Walker, 1983
Norby's Other Secret (with Janet Asimov) Walker, 1984
Norby and the Last Princess (with Janet Asimov) Walker, 1985
Norby and the Invaders (with Janet Asimov) Walker, 1985
Norby and the Queen's Necklace (with Janet Asimov) Walker, 1986
Norby Finds a Villain (with Janet Asimov) Walker, 1987
Norby Down to Earth (with Janet Asimov) Walker, 1988
Norby and Yobo's Great Adventure (with Janet Asimov) Walker, 1989
Norby and the Oldest Dragon (with Janet Asimov) Walker, 1990
The Ugly Little Boy Doubleday, 1992
Norby and the Court Jester (with Janet Asimov) Walker, 1993

Science

The Realm of Measure Houghton Mifflin, 1961
The Human Body Houghton Mifflin, 1963
Satellites In Outer Space Random House, 1964
The Clock We Live On Harper & Row, 1965
Environments Out There Harper & Row, 1967
Great Ideas of Science Houghton Mifflin, 1969
What Make the Sun Shine? Little, Brown, 1971
Inside the Atom Harper & Row, 1974
Alpha Centauri, the Nearest Star Lothrop, Lee & Shepard, 1976
How Did We Find Out About _____? (series) Walker, 1973-1990

History

    Greeks: A Great Adventure Houghton Mifflin, 1965

    The Dark Ages Houghton Mifflin, 1968

    The Land of Canaan Houghton Mifflin, 1971

    The Shaping of North America Houghton Mifflin, 1973

    The Birth of the United States Houghton Mifflin, 1974

    Animals of the Bible Doubleday, 1978

Language

    Words of Science Houghton Mifflin, 1959

    Words from the Myths Houghton Mifflin, 1961

    Words on the Map Houghton Mifflin, 1962

Edited or Written With Others

    Tomorrow's TV Raintree Publishers, 1981

    Fantastic Creatures Raintree Publishers, 1981

    After the End Raintree Publishers, 1981

    Earth Invaded Raintree Publishers, 1982

    Hallucination Orbit: Psychology in Science Fiction Farrar, Straus &
Giroux, 1983

Timeline

1920—Born in Petrovichi, Russia

1923—Family emigrates to New York City

1935—Graduates from senior high to Seth Low Junior College

1937—Graduates from Seth Low Junior College to Columbia University.

Begins "Cosmic Corkscrew," first science-fiction story

1938—Completes and submits "Cosmic Corkscrew."

Meets John Campbell.

1939—Graduates from undergraduate school to graduate school at Columbia University

1941—Submits "Foundation" to Campbell

1942—Qualifies as Ph.D. candidate at Columbia University.

Begins work at Philadelphia Navy Yard.

Marries Gertrude Blugerman.

1945—Drafted into Army.

1946—Discharged from Army.

Returns to graduate school at Columbia University.

1948—Earns Ph.D in Biochemistry.

1949—Begins instructorship at Boston University.

Doubleday accepts book-length manuscript "Grow Old With Me." Later published under title *Pebble in the Sky.*

1950—Begins focusing on writing nonfiction, first articles and then book-length works

1951—Birth of son David.
1955—Birth of daughter Robyn.
1956—Asimovs purchase home in West Newton, Massachusetts.
1958—Stops teaching at Boston University and begins writing full-time.
1963—Wins the Hugo for essays published in *The Magazine of Fantasy and Science Fiction.*
1966—Wins Hugo for Foundation series
1970—Separates from Gertrude and moves to New York City
1973—Divorce becomes final and marries Janet Jeppson.
1976—Publication of first issue of *Isaac Asimov's Science Fiction Magazine.*
Wins Hugo for his story "The Bicentennial Man."
1977—Hospitalized with heart trouble
1987—Wins Nebula for life's work
1990—Finishes memoir *I. Asimov*
1992—Death due to kidney failure

Glossary

academic	having to do with school coursework
archives	places in which historical records or public documents are preserved.
catechol	compound used in dyeing and tanning.
chloroform	treat with toxin to produce death.
congestive	causing excessive fullness of blood in blood vessels.
copyright	exclusive legal right to reproduce, publish, and sell a literary work.
deferment	official postponement of military service.
dialog	conversation between individuals.
dissect	cut open to examine.
dissertation	written treatment of a subject.
diuretics	medicines to increase the flow of urine through the body, relieving the body of excess fluid.
eccentric	strange, weird, not normal.
enzyme	protein that is produced by living cells and that catalyzes biochemical reactions.
fantasy	imaginative fiction containing strange settings and grotesque characters.
immigrants	foreigners moving into a new country.
induction	procedure by which a civilian is taken into military service.

ironically	having the opposite of the original intent or meaning.
malaria	disease caused by parasites in red blood cells, transmitted by mosquito bite.
manuscript	written or typed composition not yet in published form.
mentor	trusted counselor or guide.
mock	fake or artificial or pretend.
novellas	short novels.
Ph.D.	Doctor of Philosophy degree.
planetarium	building that contains a device for projecting celestial images and effects.
plot	story line, or what happens in a literary work
pulp	cheap paper like that used in newspapers and in the fiction magazines of the early twentieth century.
rabbi	leader in a Jewish synagogue.
retentive	having the power to retain or remember.
tenure	status granted to teacher which protects him/her from being fired.

Bibliography

Asimov, Isaac. 1994. *I. Asimov: A Memoir.* New York: Doubleday.

Asimov, Isaac. 1989. *Asimov's Galaxy: Reflections on Science Fiction.* New York: Doubleday.

Asimov, Isaac. 1974. *Before the Golden Age.* New York: Doubleday.

Asimov, Isaac. 1972. *The Early Asimov.* New York: Doubleday.

Asimov, Isaac. 1980. *In Joy Still Felt: The Autobiography of Isaac Asimov, 1954-1978.* Garden City, NY: Doubleday & Company.

Asimov, Isaac. 1979. *In Memory Yet Green: The Autobiography of Isaac Asimov, 1920-1954.* New York: Doubleday.

Asimov, Stanley (Ed.) 1995 *Yours, Isaac Asimov.* New York: Doubleday.

Erlanger, Ellen. 1986. *Isaac Asimov: Scientist and Storyteller.* Minneapolis: Lerner Publications Company.

Fiedler, Jean and Mele, Jim. 1982. *Isaac Asimov.* New York: Frederick Unger Publishing Company.

Gunn, James. 1982. *Isaac Asimov: The Foundations of Science Fiction.* New York: Oxford University Press.

Olander, Joseph D. and Greenberg, Martin Harry (Ed.). 1977. *Isaac Asimov.* New York: Taplinger Publishing Co.

Panshin, Alexei and Cory. 1989. *The World Beyond the Hill: Science Fiction and the Quest for Transcendence.* Los Angeles, CA: Jeremy P. Tarcher, Inc.

Patrouch, Jr., Joseph E. 1974. *The Science Fiction of Isaac Asimov.* Garden City, NY: Doubleday and Co., Inc.

Sources

CHAPTER ONE
"Isaac can find..." Asimov, Isaac. *In Memory Yet Green*. Garden City, NY: Doubleday, 1979. p. 49.
"Isaac, where did you..." Asimov, op.cit., p. 21.
"Stop fighting..." Asimov, Isaac. *I. Asimov*. New York: Bantam Books, 1994, p. 9
"Are you going..." Asimov, Isaac. *In Memory Yet Green*. Garden City, NY: Doubleday, 1979, p. 57.
"talked a little..." Asimov, op.cit., p. 74.
"for keeps" Asimov, Isaac. *I. Asimov*. New York: Bantam Books, 1994, p. 30.

CHAPTER TWO
"it was the..." Asimov, op. cit., p.136.
"Well this is..." Asimov, op. cit., p. 156.
"...except one..." Asimov, op. cit., pp. 160-161.
"Serve you right..." Asimov, op. city., p. 172.
"Why is it..." Asimov, op. cit., p. 173.
"If I had..." Asimov, op. cit., p. 173.

CHAPTER THREE
"What I wanted..." Asimov, op. cit., p. 192.
"Mr. Campbell will..." Asimov, op. cit., p. 194
"At 9:30 I..." Asimov, op. cit., p. 197.
"...it was the nicest..." Asimov, op.cit., p. 201.
"Oh, yes, your..." Asimov, op. cit., p. 263.
"cleverest" Asimov, op. cit., p. 266.

"That was mean..." Asimov, op. cit., p. 266.

"Heartbreak..." Asimov, Isaac. *I. Asimov*. New York: Bantam Books, 1994. pp. 96-97.

"Asimov, when you..." Asimov, Isaac. *In Memory Yet Green*. Garden City, NY: Doubleday, 1979, p. 281.

"1. A robot may..." Asimov, op. cit., p.286.

"go home and write the outline..." Asimov, op. cit., p. 311.

"...I'm not in..." Asimov, op. cit., pp. 316-317.

"Pappa! Pappa!" Asimov, op. cit., p. 323.

"Go home and write a story..." Asimov. op. cit., p. 327.

CHAPTER FOUR

"she was five..." Asimov, op. cit., pp. 330-331.

"I was the..." Asimov, op. cit., p. 435.

"I can't change...." Asimov, op. cit., p. 432.

"Who appointed you..." Asimov, op. cit., p.458

"See here..." Asimov op. cit., p. 491.

"What is *M*?" Asimov, op. cit., p. 509.

"Hey, that was..." Asimov, op. cit., p. 518.

"So what?" Asimov, op. cit., 525.

"What can you..." Asimov, op. cit., p. 526.

"Congratulations..." Asimov, op. cit., 526.

CHAPTER FIVE

"Who cares..." Asimov, op. cit., p. 550.

"Do you know..." Asimov, op. cit., pp. 576-577.

"Pardon me..." Asimov, op. cit., p. 581.

"Last night I..." Asimov, op. cit., p. 582.

"Anywhere..." Asimov, op. cit., pp. 611-612.

"Gertrude did not..." Asimov, op. cit., p. 616.

"Gertrude!" Asimov, op. cit., pp. 630-631.

"Why don't you..." Asimov, op. cit., p. 636.

CHAPTER SIX

"What's your name?" Asimov, Isaac. *In Joy Still Felt*. Garden City, NY: Doubleday, 1980. pp. 65-66.

"So what are you..." Asimov. op, cit., pp. 73-74.

CHAPTER SEVEN
"This school cannot..." Asimov, _I. Asimov._ New York: Bantam Books, 1994. p. 198.

"Yes, I do..." Asimov, Isaac. _In Joy Still Felt._ Garden City, NY: Doubleday, 1980. pp. 192-193.

"Maybe you can..." Asimov, op. cit., pp. 220-221.

"Daddy, do you..." Asimov, op. cit., p. 221.

"Which of these..." Asimov, op. cit., pp. 305-306.

"putting science in..." Asimov, op. cit., p. 318.

"Lately I've been..." Asimov, op. cit., p. 354.

"Isaac Asimov for..." Asimov, op. cit., p. 406

"Does this mean..." Asimov, op. cit., pp. 370-371

CHAPTER EIGHT
"Why don't you..." Asimov, op. cit., p. 418.

"My father will be..." Asimov, op. cit., p. 418.

"I don't suppose..." Asimov, Isaac. _I. Asimov._ New York: Bantam Books, 1994. p. 257.

"I had made my..." Asimov, Isaac. _In Joy Still Felt._ Garden City, NY: Doubleday, 1980. p. 594.

"Doctor, Doctor..." Asimov, Isaac. _I. Asimov._ New York: Bantam Books, 1994. p. 358.

"I'm sorry..." Asimov, Isaac. _In Joy Still Felt._ Garden City, NY: Doubleday, 1980. p. 610.

"Listen!" Asimov, op. cit., pp. 610-611.

"I feel as though..." Asimov, op. cit., p. 661.

CHAPTER NINE
"Being interviewed..." Asimov, op. cit., p. 695.

"What if the..." Asimov, op. cit., pp. 706-707.

"Do you think..." Asimov, op. cit., p. 709.

"What is this.." Asimov, Isaac. _I. Asimov._ New York: Bantam Books, 1994. pp. 267-268.

"Girls, feeding you..." Asimov, Isaac. _In Joy Still Felt._ Garden City, NY: 1980. p. 722.

"Dear Dr. Asimov..." Asimov, op. cit., p. 739.

"In this autobiography..." Asimov, _I. Asimov._ New York: Bantam Books,

1994. p. 443.

"Make me up a..." Asimov, op.cit., pp. 495-496.

"I made it..." Asimov, op. cit., p. 560.

"It has always..." Asimov, op. cit., p. 561.

"I want..." Asimov, op. cit., pp. 561-562.

"Isaac, you're..." Asimov, op. cit., p. 562.

"I love..." Asimov, op. cit., p. 561.

"Over a space of..." Asimov, op. cit., p. 562.

"...it is my opinion... Asimov, op. cit., p. 446.

Index